ALL THINGS
TO ALL PEOPLE

From the library of

ALL THINGS
TO ALL PEOPLE

• • • • • •

A Catholic Church
for the Twenty-First Century

• • • • • •

Louis DeThomasis, FSC

in extenso

ALL THINGS TO ALL PEOPLE
A Catholic Church for the Twenty-First Century
by Louis DeThomasis, FSC

Edited by Gregory F. Augustine Pierce
Cover and text design and typesetting by Patricia A. Lynch, Harvest Graphics

Cover illustration "All Are Welcome" © Br. Mickey McGrath, OSFS.
Used with permission.

Published by In Extenso Press
Distributed exclusively by ACTA Publications, 4848 N. Clark Street,
Chicago, IL 60640, (800) 397-2282, www.actapublications.com

Library of Congress Catalog Number: 2016933738
Paperback ISBN: 978-0-87946-985-6
Printed in the United States of America by Total Printing Systems
Year 25 24 23 22 21 20 19 18 17 16
Printing 15 14 13 12 11 10 9 8 7 6 5 4 3 2 First

♻ Text printed on 30% post-consumer recycled paper

CONTENTS

INTRODUCTION

Still Christ's Church,
But Reimagined for Today

· · · · · ·

I have become all things to all people,
that I might by all means save some.
I do it all for the sake of the gospel,
so that I may share in its blessings.

1 CORINTHIANS 9:22-23, NRSV

· · · · · ·

Paul's description of himself as a follower and evangelizer of Jesus Christ is someone who becomes "all things to all people…for the sake of the gospel." That's right. According to Paul, to do anything less is not giving our all. Therefore, even two thousand years later, the church, its leaders, and all of Jesus' followers must be held to this difficult standard. Nothing less than becoming "all things to all people" is acceptable.

Becoming "all things to all people," however, isn't obvious or easy. In some ways it smacks of moral relativism or cafeteria Catholicism, two of the biggest bugaboos in the church today. In some ways, it is so difficult to accomplish that it seems easier just to do the opposite: State the truth as we know it as absolute and let the chips fall where they may. It seems that even Paul struggled with this "all things to all people" approach, but he did it "for the sake of the Gospel."

And so, my friends, must we. If someone needs us to be conservative, we must be conservative. If they need moderation, we must be right smack in the middle. If they need progressive, then progressive we will be.

Even if at times the observations that follow may seem quite critical (or certainly at least impolitic or undiplomatic, given the clashes and tensions in the church today) I think it's about time that the People of God find the courage to speak *out* to all Jesus' followers and to all people of good faith, and to speak *up* to all institutional church leaders forcefully, although always with Christian love. Love for the church does not preclude criticism of or about the church. If we are to become "one" in the church (as we pray every day in the Creed), it seems to me to be indisputable—whether we are conservative, moderate, or progressive by nature—that we desperately need to increase our knowledge and understanding of the gospel, the good news of Jesus Christ, in a caring, supportive, and loving Christian spirit.

> • • • • • •
>
> *There are just too many in the church today who still believe that they have a monopoly on what is the "one true church."*
>
> • • • • • •

It is unfortunate that we do not seem to have that spirit now, even in the gently challenging pontificate of Pope Francis. There are just too many in the church today who still believe that they have a monopoly on what is the "one true church." And yes, as you read this book I can understand if you contend that my directness makes me guilty of that same monopolistic spirit. My hope, though, is that you will not confuse my criticisms for disrespect but rather see them as my desire to encourage honesty, reverence, and loyalty in the Catholic Church that I have been honored to be part of my entire life and that I still serve as a De LaSalle Christian Brother.

I state from the outset that I am firmly convinced that the problem for the church today is not that there are those who are conservative and those who are moderates and those who are progressive. When in the two-thousand-year history of the church was there unanimity of thought and persuasion among the faithful or even the hierarchy? My reading is that the serious difficulties the church finds itself in today are because of the fringe ideologues on both sides. (By the way, that is the same problem in other faith traditions also, and that is the cause of the current horrors of terrorism under the waving banners of "We Know God's Will and You Don't.")

When people honestly seek knowledge and understanding about the Catholic Church and the Christian faith, often times there can be good, deep, and sustained (heated?) debate. Though unintended, there can also enter into that debate some inevitable confusion, questioning, and doubt. Bewilderment often becomes apparent when this discussion takes place between academic theologians and interested and concerned Catholics who are not professional theologians.

Today, however, there are many professional theologians who reflect Pope Francis' insight that he shared in 2015 to the theology faculty on the occasion of the 100th anniversary of the Pontifical Catholic University of Argentina: "The good theologians, like the good shepherds, smell of the people and of the road and, with their reflection, pour oil and wine on the wounds of humankind." Yet when many of today's theologians are responsive to the faithful by using sensitive, compassionate, and less rigid traditional theology to try to heal the "wounds of humankind," they are criticized, condemned, even disciplined.

Even in this time of Pope Francis, church bureaucrats are still demanding orthodox loyalty oaths of teachers and staffs and are restricting Catholic colleges and high schools in their approaches as they respond to their students' religious and spiritual concerns. The unintended result is that these students seek answers from sources outside the church and the Catholic schools. Such interference from the institutional church impedes professional, dedicated, and caring Catholic schoolteachers and professors from accompanying students on their faith journeys in today's pluralistic and globalized world.

In my recent book, *The Dynamics of Catholic Education: Letting the Catholic School Be School*, I observed: "The institutional church, for its part, must extend its encouragement and support to the Catholic school with the same understanding that it has publicly professed when it mandates that we should teach as Jesus did, who said: 'Whoever welcomes one such child in my name welcomes me'" (Mark 9:37, *NRSV*).

Even though many theologians and teachers are placed in an untenable position by tension between what is allowed and what they know needs to be said, the situation continues to persist. This friction is especially prevalent for those who have adapted modern day scientific knowledge and insights into their writings and integrated Pope Francis' more pastoral approach into their theological presentations.

It is proper and considerate that we all turn off our cell phones when we enter a church, but it should not be mandatory for us to turn off our brains as well. Perhaps, we should all heed the advice of Zachary R. Dehm, who wrote in the *National Catholic Reporter's* "Young Voices" column (November 6, 2014):

> *Theologians need strangers. If we do not engage strangers in theological discussion, we limit ourselves to only engaging other professional theologians. We insulate theology in the comfortable walls of our vocabulary and ideas. Without constant connection to those living the Christian (or non-Christian) life through their own vocation, we lose contact with the subject of our theologizing. We lose a fundamental perspective for doing theology, which we need if we are going to do our task well. To do good theology, we have to be willing to talk to strangers, even when the universe brings them to us randomly and without invitation.*

I write this book not as a professional theologian—which I am not—but as a faithful member of the church I love. It is my belief that more than ever in the church there is still a significant and more urgent need to transform how we are a church today in a world that has seen a globalized transformation of people and societies. We must become all things to all people, and people are more varied today than they were even at the time of the Second Vatican Council. More and more people—especially young people—are judging that many of the current leaders in the church, even those supporting Pope Francis' efforts, simply refuse to transform their ways so they can protect the status quo, including their powers and perks of office.

An observation (*NCR*, Nov. 14, 2014) by Thomas Reese, SJ, about the U.S. Conference of Catholic Bishops' November 2014 Baltimore meeting gives us an insight into why we must continue and repeat a call for transformation in the Catholic Church. Father Reese wrote:

> *A lack of passion and leadership marked the meeting of the U.S. Conference of Catholic Bishops this week in Baltimore. Their agenda was stale and did not reflect the excitement that Pope Francis' papacy has generated.*
>
> *A big part of the trouble with the American hierarchy is that the bishops have no one to consult. The conservative theologians, who have been advising them during the last two papacies, are as upset as the ideologically conservative bishops. Since progressive theologians were labeled heretics, kicked out of seminaries, and shunned like Ebola patients, bishops have no one to explain to them how to thrive with the discussion and debate being encouraged by Francis.*

In the opening to this Introduction, I chose an essential insight into the nature of Christianity that Paul shared with the faithful: "I have become all things to all people, that I might by all means save some. I do it all for the sake of the gospel, so that I may share in its blessings." A poignant understanding of the richness and power of that same passage is well captured in the wonderful modern Scripture translation by Eugene Peterson:

Even though I am free of the demands and expectations of everyone, I have voluntarily become a servant to any and all in order to reach a wide range of people: religious, nonreligious, meticulous moralists, loose-living immoralists, the defeated, the demoralized—whoever. I didn't take on their way of life. I kept my bearings in Christ—but I entered their world and tried to experience things from their point of view. I've become just about every sort of servant there is in my attempts to lead those I meet into a God-saved life. I did all this because of the Message. I didn't just want to talk about it; I wanted to be in on it!

1 Corinthians 9:19-25, *The Message*

As a longstanding member of the De LaSalle Christian Brothers; as one who is striving with all my imperfections, sins, and shortcomings to become a more dedicated and committed faithful follower of Jesus Christ; and as a proud and loyal member of the Catholic Church—I feel compelled to be honest and share with you my concerns and my dreams for the church I love. I, too, want "to be in on" this important discussion about the future of the church, and in doing so I believe it is essential that I try to speak to everyone, for everyone, and about everyone in the true spirit of Paul's declaration.

This necessarily compels me to be candid and honest about my interpretations as to what I see happening in our church today. I write this book trying to, in the words of *The Message*, "become a servant to any and all in order to reach a wide range of people: religious, nonreligious, meticulous moralists, loose-living immoralists, the defeated, the demoralized...." I am totally prepared to accept that not all will agree with what I am saying, but I will "attempt to be all things to all people" so that no one will be confused as to what I am saying.

In a recent book I co-authored with Sister Cynthia Nienhaus, CSA, *The Silent Schism: Healing the Serious Split in the Catholic Church,* we stated that all of the faithful through the power of the Holy Spirit are called to be prophets in the sense that we must make Jesus' words of two thousand years ago meaningful for us today. But to do this, we wrote:

As the prophetic People of God, we must be there for the saints and the sinners; for the orthodox and the unorthodox; for the married and the divorced; for the straights and the gays; for the conservatives and the liberals; for the women who, in the sanctity of their conscience, believe they are called to be priests and deacons in the Catholic church. We must stand on the side of the oppressed, just as Jesus always did.

I do not see my contribution to this dialogue as something frivolous or without purpose. I take seriously the idea of visions and dreams as revealed in the Old Testament in Numbers 12:6: "Hear my words: When there are prophets among you, I the Lord make myself known to them in visions; I speak to them in dreams."

Please understand that in no manner am I suggesting that I am a prophet. (In fact, if you were to ask my confreres in the De LaSalle Brothers, they would have many choice words to describe me, and none of those descriptors would even begin with the letter "p.") But I am convinced that many of the faithful today are seeing visions and having dreams of a more inclusive, welcoming, and relevant church. Together, we are all prophets of a new heaven and a new earth. Together we see visions. Together we have dreams. This book is an attempt to unfold and reveal those graced visions. I believe that the faithful must share our dreams and visions of the future church. I dream of a future church that includes all; a church that accepts each person at the point that each stands on his or her spiritual journey; a church that understands the real struggles and doubts of all people.

Louis DeThomasis, FSC, PhD
Rome, Italy
Easter Sunday 2016

CHAPTER 1

A Small Word, But with a Big Impact

• • • • • •

"Go and learn what this means, 'I desire mercy, not sacrifice.'
For I have come to call not the righteous but sinners."

MATTHEW 9:12-13, NRSV

• • • • • •

The small word—*but*—can make all the difference when we try to understand what people mean when they attempt to tell us something, especially something important, even life-changing. It is not an insignificant three-letter word that merely fills in a brief pause in a sentence. *But* has distinctive meanings depending on how it is used in a sentence. Many times it clarifies an entire thought or idea.

For example, in the words from the Gospel of Matthew above, Jesus is driving home to his disciples (us) that his ministry, his mission, his vocation, his very purpose, was to reach out to those who are estranged from God, not to those who are right with God. Eugene Peterson translates the passage this way:

"Who needs a doctor: the healthy or the sick? Go figure out what this Scripture means: 'I'm after mercy, not religion.' I'm here to invite outsiders, not coddle insiders."

Matthew 9:12-13, *The Message*

If you survey various dictionaries and word-source reference materials, you will see many meanings and uses for the word *but* (and its longer cousin, *however*). At times *but* is used as a conjunction in a sentence and conveys a sense of "yet," "except," "unless," "otherwise," etc. For instance: *She was so sad that she could do nothing but pray for a better life.* Sometimes *but* can be used as a preposition and convey the idea of an exception. An example would be: *No one follows the rules but me.* The word *but* may also be used as an adverb, as in: *There is but one God.* Or as a noun, as in: *Follow the rules, and no buts about it.*

In essence *but* commonly conveys something that is either in opposition or contrast to something else. It highlights an idea that signals to the listener "in spite of" or "nevertheless" or something "further" that must be understood. It implies there is another item that is equally true or an additional point that must certainly be taken into consideration. For instance: *I am leaving, but I will return.*

Because of the nuanced understandings of this small three-letter word, it is intriguing to explore its significance on the dynamics of the Catholic faith today.

Should today's church, the current People of God (as we call ourselves) see a graced potentiality for a better understanding of the Word of God when we explore how *but* is used in Scripture? Does this small word have the power to light up the horizons of Christianity for the twenty-first century, helping us to discern the whole truth, spirit and beauty of Jesus' Good News? In other words, when we read the Bible or study theology, does it impose on us a sense of a rigid, unequivocal, and permanent set of facts being legislated or does it announce a living, transforming, expansive spiritual truth?

For example, when we reflect on Jesus as he ushered into the world the

Good News of our salvation, are we not in awe that he was as human as you or me but still, as Catholics believe, was so intertwined with the reality of his Father in heaven that he himself was divine? The Catholic faith teaches that Jesus was not just pretending to be human but was truly God and truly human. That's a truth of our faith, but it is not a scientifically verifiable fact. (You can see that just in this paragraph, without the use of the word *but* we Catholics could not adequately explain some of the basic truths of our faith.)

So, here we are. Even though there are volumes upon volumes of theological, philosophical, doctrinal, catechetical, and dogmatic texts explaining Jesus and his message, we know that no amount of words or human reasoning can capture his reality and meaning for today. Without that little word *but*, we can never fully understand the truth of who Jesus really was, and continues to be, for us.

When Catholics and other Christians proclaim in the Nicene Creed that "We believe in one, holy, catholic, and apostolic church," we are saying that for over two thousand years the church—in spite of the weaknesses, mistakes, and scandals—is truly one, holy, catholic (note the small "c"), and apostolic, but we also know there have always been sinners inside the church. Without that wonderful word *but*, we can never fully explain this mystery.

I am not saying that attempts to explain the doctrine and dogma of the faith should be relative (one the one hand, but on the other hand). To the contrary, I am saying that it is only by using the word *but* that we can adequately be "all things to all people." Let's not kid ourselves. (We are certainly not fooling anyone else!) We Catholics must completely acknowledge that no one person (even the pope), no magisterium, no curia, no bishop, and no theology will ever be able to fully explain the Good News in terms of verifiable human/ scientific facts. At Mass, we Catholics proclaim what we call *the Mystery of Faith:* "Christ has died. Christ is risen. Christ will come again." This can only be understood as a paradox and a metaphor. Therefore, should not our doctrines, dogma, rules, and pronouncements also reflect this truth of our faith? We are a church reliant on the word *but* to explain our beliefs.

It is the Holy Spirit, inspiring the People of God over time, who reveals to the faithful the endless and evolving truth of the divine mystery—not scientific formulas, facts, doctrines, and rules. Let us not forget even St. Thomas Aquinas observed. "Life itself is prior to doctrine."

Do we have to remind ourselves of one of the most famous historical blunders of the church, one in which it confused scientific facts with the deeper truth of the faith? It was the Roman Inquisition in 1615 that forbade Galileo Galilei to advocate the scientific fact of *heliocentrism*, i.e., that the earth revolved around the sun. The church at the time taught that the earth was the center of the universe and that all heavenly bodies revolved around the earth. The Inquisition insisted that if Galileo did not agree with the facts that they taught he would be declared a heretic. Galileo, facing torture, recanted. (Galileo was quoted to have said privately on his way out of the trial, "And yet it moves," referring to the planet Earth.)

Jesus' attitude toward people who, like Galileo, are not considered compliant to authority's version of the facts is quite different. At the opening of this chapter I recalled the verse in Matthew 9 that involved the incident when the Pharisees saw Jesus eating in Matthew's house and they questioned the disciples why their teacher ate with tax collectors and sinners. This seemed to annoy Jesus, and he responded, "Those who are well have no need of a physician, but those who are sick. Go and learn what this means, 'I desire mercy, not sacrifice.' For I have come to call not the righteous but sinners" (Matthew 9:12-13, *NRSV*).

Richard Beck, a psychologist who insightfully interfaces social psychology with theology, wrote *Unclean: Meditations on Purity, Hospitality, and Morality.* Using his extensive research on everyday human experiences, he thoughtfully presents fascinating theological reflection on the statement in Matthew 9:13 "I desire mercy, not sacrifice."

Beck takes as his foundation for his observations the works of Walter Brueggemann and Fernando Belo and their research on the two prevalent yet antagonistic visions at that time in Israel's history, i.e. the understanding of "uprightness before God." The two opposing forces were: (1) the Levitical or "priestly vision," and (2) the Prophetic or "justice vision." The Levitical direction of "uprightness before God" emphasized the necessity for cultic purity for all and gave very detailed rules for how people were to act in almost every situation. However, the Prophetic approach focused on concern and care for the poor, the needy, and the marginalized. Before Jesus comes on the scene, these two opposing views of life were continuously present, resulting in much animosity among the Jewish faithful (sound familiar?).

There is no doubt where Jesus stands.... His God demands inclusion of all, not exclusion of anyone.

Now comes Jesus, who was being severely criticized by the Pharisees for mingling, associating, and even eating with the despised tax collectors and sinners. After reading Matthew 9, there is no doubt where Jesus stands on the Levitical-Prophetic divide. His God demands *inclusion* of all, not *exclusion* of anyone. Jesus makes clear the unequivocal Christian message by opting for the Prophetic vision of Judaism. To follow him means that no one—especially the sinner—is to be looked upon with disgust. All of us are embraced in the unconditional love of the Lord. That's the Christian truth, one that no doctrinal words or facts will ever be able to fully explain.

In an interview with Chris Keller published in *The Other Journal: An Intersection of Theology and Culture* on February 16, 2012, Beck had a powerful and pointed observation to make about this when he said:

Here's how all this plays out psychologically: My sense is that a lot of churches think they can have it both ways. You often see this in the common refrain "love the sinner but hate the sin." The psychological research I review in Unclean *suggests that this maxim is almost impossible to put into practice. Psychologically speaking, mercy and purity pull us in opposite directions. And behaviorally, as we see in Matthew 9, we have to make a choice: follow Jesus as he crosses the purity boundary or stand with the Pharisees who have opted for quarantine.*

Without Jesus using that short, innocent-looking word *but* when bluntly telling the Pharisees that he, the Son of God, came to earth not just for the righteous but the sinner, what chance would any of us have for salvation? That simple, single "but" uttered by Jesus captures and embraces the mystery of the Catholic faith.

Facts and truths are simply not the same thing. Niels Bohr, a 1922 winner of the Nobel Prize for Physics, captured this distinction when he insightfully observed: *"The opposite of a fact is falsehood, but the opposite of one profound truth may very well be another profound truth."*

Truth is a reality that is not simply understood with data. It must be discovered, lived, revealed. In the theological sense, truth involves a fundamental and transcendent reality that goes beyond any theology, philosophy, or laws.

No human controls, and no church authority, can stop the revelation of truth about God and the church. Human words, doctrines, or canons of laws are not the keys that open the doors to sanctity; rather, it is our personal experience and relationship with the Lord, encountered within our hearts and imaginations.

It is not in the recitation of words in prayers that makes us holy, but rather it is living a prayerful life, i.e. a life animated by living in the presence of the one true God and acting with love in all that we do.

I dream of a church that embraces the truth that the Holy Spirit inspires all the faithful to discern God's will. I dream that the Holy Spirit's inspiration will make us all free to bring our doubts, disagreements, and questions to the conversation. Jesus always calls us to "Come follow me," not "Come obey my rules."

CHAPTER 2

Imagine a Beautiful, But Messy, Church

• • • • • •

*I'm doing everything that I can, working with experts,
really studying the statistics to figure out a way
we can make it cool or normal to be kind and loving.*

Lady Gaga

• • • • • •

Lady Gaga is an unexpected source given the usual nature of our discussion about the Catholic Church. But she has given some good advice to the young people she is trying to help in her foundation, named *Born This Way.* She said, "I work very hard, but when God opens that door for you—when life opens that door for you, I should say—I think it's important to be giving, to return the love back." It may be that this secular pop icon may be using a non-sacramental symbol for God's grace—an opening door. And she sees that a true response to a loving God opening a door is not commanding, controlling, and proclaiming with rigid and prescribed dictums, but "giving" and "loving back."

At the Mass just before the 2005 Papal Conclave that chose him as pope, Cardinal Joseph Ratzinger, who shortly became Pope Benedict XVI, used the term *"dictatorship of relativism."* He used this term to describe what he interpreted as a growing secularism taking over society that does not accept anything as definitive or universally true. Such relativism holds that everything is subjective and culturally conditioned without any universally valid standard.

I am convinced, however, that a culture insisting that everyone follow prescribed standards in lock step as a requirement for Christianity is just as dangerous as, or perhaps more dangerous than, Pope Benedict's obsessive fear of a *"dictatorship of relativism."*

Is there some biblical foundation to my premise that love, not rules and absolutes, is how Christianity should respond when God opens a door? Consider the text in Acts 10, especially verses 23 to 48, the story of Peter and Cornelius, the Roman officer who becomes the first Gentile follower of Christ. I believe we are presented here with an undeniable manifestation of the essential mechanism by which Christianity has flourished. The story challenges the idea that the church should be a fortress for legalistic regulators forcing rigid conformity. Peter is about to become "all things to all people." Without Cornelius and the dynamics that overcame dissension about his acceptance into the beginning Christian church as a non-Jew, Christianity might consist only of those who followed all Jewish customs and laws.

• • • • • •

Without Cornelius and the dynamics that overcame dissension about his acceptance into the beginning Christian church as a non-Jew, Christianity might consist only of those who followed all Jewish customs and laws.

• • • • • •

Acts relates the distress—perhaps even the obsessive fear—that Peter had when he went to Cornelius' house and a crowd of Gentiles greeted him. Peter knew that he would be severely criticized for associating with Gentiles. After all they were not Jews; they were the uncircumcised; they did not go to the Temple; they ate all the forbidden and unclean animals; furthermore, Jewish law declared that just associating with "those people" was unlawful for any Jew. But Cornelius had sent for him and Peter, to his credit, went. The placement and length of this story in the Acts of the Apostles show how pivotal the event was to the early church.

When Peter arrives at Cornelius' house, Cornelius says to him, *"So now all of us are here in the presence of God to listen to all that the Lord has commanded you to say*" (verse 33, *NRSV*). Peter states: *"I truly understand that God shows no partiality, but in every nation anyone who fears him and does what is right is acceptable to him"* (verses 34-35, *NRSV*). We see with this utterance of an emphatic "but" in Peter's declaration that the rock upon which Jesus built his church (and the universally proclaimed first pope) is the one who engineers a major transformation of the Christian faith.

Eugene Peterson translates the story this way. Note the "but there it was" near the end:

The next morning Peter got up and went with them. Some of his friends from Joppa went along. A day later they entered Caesarea. Cornelius was expecting them and had his relatives and close friends waiting with him. The minute Peter came through the door, Cornelius was up on his feet greeting him—and then down on his face worshiping him! Peter pulled him up and said, "None of that—I'm a man and only a man, no different from you."

Talking things over, they went on into the house, where Cornelius introduced Peter to everyone who had come. Peter addressed them, "You know, I'm sure that this is highly irregular. Jews just don't do this—visit and relax with people of another race. But God has just shown me that no race is better than any other. So the minute I was sent for, I came, no questions asked. But now I'd like to know why you sent for me."

Cornelius said, "Four days ago at about this time, midafternoon, I was home praying. Suddenly there was a man right in front of me, flooding the room with light. He said, 'Cornelius, your daily prayers and neighborly acts have brought you to God's attention. I want you to send to Joppa to get Simon, the one they call Peter. He's staying with Simon the Tanner down by the sea.'

"So I did it—I sent for you. And you've been good enough to come. And now we're all here in God's presence, ready to listen to whatever the Master put in your heart to tell us."

Peter fairly exploded with his good news: "It's God's own truth, nothing could be plainer: God plays no favorites! It makes no difference who you are or where you're from—if you want God and are ready to do as he says, the door is open. The Message he sent to the children of Israel—that through Jesus Christ everything is being put together again—well, he's doing it everywhere, among everyone.

"You know the story of what happened in Judea. It began in Galilee after John preached a total life-change. Then Jesus arrived from Nazareth, anointed by God with the Holy Spirit, ready for action. He went through the country helping people and healing everyone who was beaten down by the Devil. He was able to do all this because God was with him.

"And we saw it, saw it all, everything he did in the land of the Jews and in Jerusalem where they killed him, hung him from a cross. But in three days God had him up, alive, and out where he could be seen. Not everyone saw him—he wasn't put on public display. Witnesses had been carefully handpicked by God beforehand—us! We were the ones, there to eat and drink with him after he came back from the dead. He commissioned us to announce this in public, to bear solemn witness that he is in fact the One whom God destined as Judge of the living and dead. But we're not alone in this. Our witness that he is the means to forgiveness of sins is backed up by the witness of all the prophets."

No sooner were these words out of Peter's mouth than the Holy Spirit came on the listeners. The believing Jews who had come with Peter couldn't believe it, couldn't believe that the gift of the Holy Spirit was poured out on "outsider" non-Jews, but there it was—they heard them speaking in tongues, heard them praising God.

Then Peter said, "Do I hear any objections to baptizing these friends with water? They've received the Holy Spirit exactly as we did." Hearing no objections, he ordered that they be baptized in the name of Jesus Christ.

Then they asked Peter to stay on for a few days.

Acts 10: 23-48, *The Message*

God is not partial to any nation, society, or culture. The church is "universal." It is "catholic." It is "world-wide." (And if we ever make contact with aliens from another planet, its mission and message will most certainly be for them as well.) Does that make God a relativist? I think not. God is the one God of all, the God who loves unconditionally. Does this acceptance and openness to all make the church a little messy? Of course it does. Wonderfully so! Indeed, this universality is an essential theological concept, without which there would be no Christianity as proclaimed by Jesus, who told us in no uncertain terms to preach the Good News to all nations. He did not mention anything about people having to become Jews or Romans. This could not have been said any better than Pope Francis put it during his visit to Florence, November 10, 2015: "The Lord poured out his blood not for some, not for a few or the many, but for all."

It seems obvious to me that the truth is the Christian faith is not relativistic, but it also seems obvious to me that the human words, images, and facts that describe divine truth are subject to cultural diversity and a plurality of different and graced ways of understanding that mystery. (I guess Peter may have been accused of being a "cafeteria Jew"!) Though I am certainly influenced by a Vatican II understanding of the church as the People of God, I contend that this acceptance of diversity should be just as true even for those who have a more traditional understanding of the Catholic faith.

Why is it then that so many Catholics fail to appreciate the pivotal and central way Jesus related to women and men? Jesus literally exploded his followers' imaginations with unconditional love so that they might help him announce and explain the Good News to the world. He never asked us to think, love, or pray within the confines of rules and laws; rather he simply asked us all to be one with his Father in as many ways as we can imagine.

Jesus never commanded us to be the same, or even to think the same or describe things in the same way. He asked us to *act* the same, by loving our neighbors as we love ourselves and as God loves us. Because of Jesus' example and teaching, our imaginations are able to embrace the reality of the Triune God. That takes imagination, not commands or controls.

But Jesus was not an institution. He was the Son of God. And, herein lies the tension that evolved over two thousand years in his church. Though he willed his church into existence and sent his Holy Spirit to guide it, there are nevertheless human elements involving people and organizational dynamics in play. Human institutional dynamics are prone by their very nature to formulate rules, regulations, and laws in order to bring clarity and control to human organizations. This becomes especially important to those who very legitimately endeavor to protect the institution.

But for the People of God, Jesus' church is infinitely more than just a human institution. The essential mystery of the church is that its essential mission is not to perpetuate its human organizational structures but rather it is to help bring about God's kingdom on earth in the way that it already is in heaven. No set of dogmas can ever accomplish that. Only a people on fire with God's love.

Therefore, while we should attempt to be good stewards of the church, we must never place that duty ahead of mercy, compassion, acceptance, and inclusion. This makes for a messy church, in a human organizational sense, but it is the true church that Jesus proclaimed and the one Peter eventually embraced.

A messy church does not make it a church under a dictatorship of relativism. It is not a church that is traditionalist or progressive or even moderate; but it is a church that is trying to be all things to all people, absorbed by and radiant with a spirit of love inviting the creative and energizing imaginations of women and men graced by the Holy Spirit to serve all, especially the poor and destitute of the world.

This view of the church could not have been better stated than it was by Pope Francis on his November 2014 visit to Turkey at the Mass he celebrated in the Cathedral of the Holy Spirit:

> *It is true that the Holy Spirit brings forth different charisms in the church, which at first glance, may seem to create disorder. Under his guidance, however, they constitute an immense richness, because the Holy Spirit is the Spirit of unity, which is not the same thing as uniformity. Only the Holy Spirit is able to kindle diversity, multiplicity and, at the same time, bring about unity. When we try to create diversity, but are closed within our own particular and exclusive ways of seeing things, we create division. When we try to create unity through our own human designs, we end up with uniformity and homogenization. If we let ourselves be led by the Spirit, however, richness, variety, and diversity will never create conflict, because the Spirit spurs us to experience variety in the communion of the church.*

I dream of a church that can be this kind of force throughout the world. I want us to model to the world how Christianity can respect the richness of diversity and bring together all women and men in love and respect, regardless of our many and obvious differences. I believe with the pope that "You can say that today we are not living an era of change but a change of era" (Pope Francis, Florence, November 10, 2015).

CHAPTER 3

The Facts and Nothing But the Facts

· · · · · ·

Facts are stubborn, but statistics are more pliable.

MARK TWAIN

· · · · · ·

The church is messy, but that's okay. Now let's get a little messier. Though I use quite a few Bible quotes and Bible statistics in this chapter, like Mark Twain I am not under the illusion that statistics prove my conclusions; rather, I am convinced that these statistics justify the suspicions that have led me to those conclusions.

Most of us are familiar with an observation attributed in Mark Twain's autobiography to nineteenth-century British Prime Minister Benjamin Disraeli: "There are three kinds of lies: lies, damned lies, and statistics." I would add a fourth and fifth: Biblical quotes and Biblical statistics.

So, up front I admit passages and statistics from the Scriptures can be helpful in understanding what the church should be about, but they can sometimes also be, shall we say, a bit shifty if you spin them unfairly. I assure you that I am not using them here to mislead anyone, but I am simultaneously stating that I only use them to assert my definitive bias for the assertions that I make.

I am trying to shed authentic scriptural light on the context of my reason for writing this book. So, I say up front and directly that I am not contending that these passages and statistics substantiate my convictions in a verifiable sense, but they can certainly focus attention on the context and tone of what is at the core of the very real and, fortunately, immutable Christian message. Let me begin.

First, we should draw our attention to one of the most recognized and powerful teaching moments in Jesus' life on earth, the Sermon on the Mount. Matthew 5:1-48 states clearly that Jesus sat down with his disciples to teach them. There can be no argument that he was not using that very moment to bring his message of just what it means to follow him, to be true to his Gospel of love. He even bluntly announces that what he is teaching them is not to be confused in any way whatsoever with the known rigidity and legalisms of the Pharisees who subscribe to justification before God by their insistence to follow the letter of the law: "For I tell you, unless your righteousness exceeds that of the scribes and Pharisees, you will never enter the kingdom of heaven" (verse 20, *NRSV*). Jesus could not have been more clear about what his intentions were.

Of course, Jesus did slant things a little bit when he made it clear that his message was not meant to negate the Law but rather to teach his followers the disposition a Christian should bring to the Law: "Do not think that I have come to abolish the law or the prophets; I have come not to abolish but to fulfill" (verse 17, *NRSV*). But how does Jesus tell his disciples to fulfill the law? We know that he did not recite a new list of "do nots," nor did he present institutional canons of legalisms. Instead, Jesus presented his magnificent exhortation that brings to light what it means to be his follower:

When Jesus saw the crowds, he went up the mountain; and after he sat down, his disciples came to him. Then he began to speak, and taught them, saying:

"Blessed are the poor in spirit, for theirs is the kingdom of heaven.

"Blessed are those who mourn, for they will be comforted.

"Blessed are the meek, for they will inherit the earth.

"Blessed are those who hunger and thirst for righteousness, for they will be filled.

"Blessed are the merciful, for they will receive mercy.

"Blessed are the pure in heart, for they will see God.

"Blessed are the peacemakers, for they will be called children of God.

"Blessed are those who are persecuted for righteousness' sake, for theirs is the kingdom of heaven.

"Blessed are you when people revile you and persecute you and utter all kinds of evil against you falsely on my account. Rejoice and be glad, for your reward is great in heaven, for in the same way they persecuted the prophets who were before you."

Matthew 5:1-12, *NRSV*

Jesus' Sermon on the Mount transforms the rigid and legalistic approach of institutional Judaism of his times. As if this were not enough, Jesus next leaves no doubt about his understanding of his—and therefore our—relationship to his Father in heaven, to the Creator, to Yahweh, to the Triune God.

• • • • • •

Jesus emphasizes to his followers that there is something that goes beyond traditional religious teaching that they need to grasp.

• • • • • •

To accomplish this, he uses that small and powerful word *but* to make it unequivocally clear, once and for all, what it means to be his faithful follower. This is as true for his church now, two thousand years later, as it was for that group of disciples sitting on a hill in Galilee, who heard it first.

Jesus does not accomplish his vision with one flat, declarative sentence. He emphasizes to his followers that there is something that goes beyond traditional religious teaching that they need to grasp. Five times he says: "You have heard that it was said…but I say to you…." And, in the last in that series of *but* statements Jesus makes his message strikingly clear:

"You have heard that it was said, 'You shall love your neighbor and hate your enemy.' But I say to you, love your enemies and pray for those who

persecute you, so that you may be children of your Father in heaven; for he makes his sun rise on the evil and on the good, and sends rain on the righteous and on the unrighteous. For if you love those who love you, what reward do you have? Do not even the tax collectors do the same? And if you greet only your brothers and sisters, what more are you doing than others? Do not even the Gentiles do the same? Be perfect, therefore, as your heavenly Father is perfect.

Matthew 5:43-48, *NRSV*

The rational fact and the spiritual truth are that Jesus teaches the core of his message by using that ever so small word *but* multiple times throughout the Gospels so that we may understand the full dimensions of his message. You may say, "Well, okay, so Jesus, true God and true man, used the word *but*, does that really have anything to say to us today about what Jesus wants from his followers? How are we supposed to be as perfect as God?

What it has to say to us is that Jesus signaled his unique and transformative message by demonstrating to us that to follow him is not a matter of reducing his message with simple, rigid dictums but of allowing our imaginations to realize the possibilities that living a life of love means. *The Message* translates verse 48 this way: "In a word, what I'm saying is, *Grow up*. You're kingdom subjects. Now live like it. Live out your God-created identity. Live generously and graciously toward others, the way God lives toward you."

A comparison of some biblical statistics with statistics from some church documents in the use of the word *but* may support my interpretation of the Sermon on the Mount. For instance, let's look at the use in the 1983 Code of Canon Law.

"Wait just a minute, Louis, hold on," you might say. "To compare Scripture to Canon Law is not an appropriate comparison. They are two completely different categories of writings." If you say that, you would be absolutely correct and justified in ignoring my statistics. After all, they are worse than damned lies!

But if we are seeking the spiritual truth of the faith there may be significant value in reviewing those comparative statistics, even though these two books exist in completely different genres. Such a comparison may help us sense a tone and reflection of the attitudes in these two very different presentations: the Bible and Canon Law. Canon Law is not a civil, penal codification of laws. Canon Law is a system of laws and principles regulating the institutional Catholic Church with regard to and for the effective accomplishment of its mission. As such, should we not justifiably expect that the context, mode, and choice of words in Canon Law at least reflect Jesus' approach, tone, and teachings regarding the Law? A statistical comparison of the use of *but* could give us an indication of how well or poorly Canon Law reflects Jesus' approach.

First, look at Scripture in its entirety. There are approximately 930,000 words in the Old and New Testaments combined, including the Deuterocanonical books. The number of times the word *but* appears hovers around 4,500, depending upon the translation. (I know, I counted each one myself!) Mathematically, this indicates that the incidence of the use of *but* is 0.48% of the total number of words in the Bible.

Contrast that to Canon Law, where we find a total of 121,271 words in 1,752 Canons. The word *but* appears here only 127 times. In Canon Law, therefore, the incidence of the use of but is a little over 0.10%. So the word *but*, a legitimate expression of contradiction, ambiguity, perplexity, and even paradox, appears in Scripture almost five times more often than in Canon Law.

Next, let us get a picture of the spirit of discourse when Jesus enters human history. By segregating the New Testament we can see if there is any significant progression in the tone that is introduced by Jesus and his followers. In the Old Testament *but* is used about 3,000 times, or 0.40%. In the New Testament there are a little more than 180,000 words in total and the word *but* is used over 1,500 times. Thus the incidence of its use in the New Testament is about 0.83%. Therefore, the frequency of the word *but* in the New Testament over the Old Testament is 207%. (It is an outstanding 830% over the frequency of its use in Canon Law. Apparently the authors of Canon Law had only a fraction of the need to use the word *but* compared to the divinely inspired authors of the Bible. I wonder why?)

At the risk of having your eyes glaze over, I will ask you to look now at an even more pertinent comparison when we compare the frequency of the use of the word but in the New Testament to its use in *The Catechism of the Catholic Church*. Wouldn't you assume that *The Catechism* should be somewhat comparable to the tone and teachings of the New Testament since it is primarily explaining the faith of the church as revealed by Jesus in his life and teachings? *The Catechism* has a total of 246,474 words and there is a use of *but* 684 times; the incidence of its use is 0.28%—higher than in the Code of Canon Law, to be sure, but still less than a third of its frequency in the New Testament

A promising spirit of transformation in the papacy of Francis is fostering a renewal of the original revelations that Jesus brought to this world. The Pope's principal thrust, his brightest promise as the leader of the church, is an attempt to restore the historical truth of the original message modeled and taught by Jesus Christ himself. Granted, Pope Francis has not officially changed any doctrines (yet), but he certainly transformed the tone and spirit of how we Catholics should embrace those doctrines in our daily lives. It may be helpful to those insisting on doctrinal changes to take into consideration Chicago Archbishop Blaise Cupich's remarks in a June 2014 interview. He said, "Pope Francis is new and yet the same." He continued by relating a potent and compelling observation he once heard: "John Paul II told us what to do; Benedict XVI told us why we should do it; Francis is telling us 'do it.'"

Quite revelatory, and in a sense corroboration of my conclusions, are recent remarks from another prominent member of the hierarchy, Cardinal Walter Kasper, a former German diocesan ordinary, a theologian, and President-Emeritus of the Pontifical Council for the Promotion of Christian Unity. In an interview he gave in Rome on September 26, 2014, he made some powerful observations about his convictions on this subject. Asked to comment on how he reads the current opposition and contrasting theological visions of many in today's institutional church life, he stated with some candor:

> I think they fear a domino effect, if you change one point all would collapse. That's their fear. This is all linked to ideology, an ideological understanding of the Gospel that it is like a penal code.
>
> But the Gospel, as the Pope said in The Joy of the Gospel, quoting Thomas Aquinas, is the gift of the Holy Spirit that lies in the soul of the faithful and operates in love. That's an entirely different understanding. The Gospel is not a museum. It is a living reality in the church and we have to walk with the whole People of God and see what the needs of the people are. Then we have to make a discernment in the light of the Gospel, which is not a code of doctrines and commandments.

America, September 29, 2014

The directness and clarity with which Cardinal Kasper speaks is quite extraordinary and refreshing for a high-positioned church prelate. Reverend Luis Leon, an Episcopal priest, made an insightful observation in a lecture series he presented at the 2014 Chautauqua Institution in upstate New York: "*But* is the key theological word of the Holy Spirit. We realize that a change has happened, and we see reality different. When we say *but*, we are using important theological language. The Holy Spirit has touched and changed you. And you have a new vision for what the world can be."

I dream of a church that will not resort to coercion to enforce the Gospel but will trust instead in the persuasive power that flows ever from the grace of Jesus's message of love for all. I dream of a church that flourishes and grows in the spirit of the Joy of the Gospel and is not controlled by a Dictatorship of the Powerful.

CHAPTER 4

But What Kind of Church
Did Jesus Really Establish?

• • • • • •

*And I tell you, you are Peter,
and on this rock I will build my church,
and the gates of Hades will not prevail against it.*

MATTHEW 16:18, *NRSV*

• • • • • •

Even most casual Catholics are quite familiar with the above Scripture passage and the significant emphasis that the Catholic Church has placed on it as justification for its organizational structures and institutional hierarchy.

If you really think about it, however, it would be almost impossible to fully account for the human elements that have contributed to the church's structural development over these past two thousand years. Jesus did not call Peter "the pope" (which comes from the Italian *papa* or "father"). Nor did Jesus elevate the eleven surviving apostles to cardinals (which comes from the Italian *cardo* or "door" and was originally made up of influential laypeople who could open important secular doors for the early church). Jesus did not set up a curia. He wouldn't have had the slightest idea what a diocese (from the old French for "a governor's jurisdiction") or a bishop (from the old English word for "high priest" and the Latin and Greek for "overseer") might be or why we might need one. Nor would he have envisioned a parish (which probably derives from the Greek for "nearby houses").

Let's face it. Jesus was a carpenter's son from a small town in a backwater of the Roman empire. He was not an ecclesiologist (an expert on church structures). He was a visionary, a savior, a teacher who experienced his deepest identity as the Son of the Living God. So to say that Jesus "founded" the Catholic Church, while true, is not true the way many church leaders would have us believe. Yes, Catholics believe that the Holy Spirit is always with the church, but that doesn't mean that the Spirit mandates certain structures or rules for the church to operate under. In fact, the opposite is true. As Vatican II pointed out, the church has to read "the signs of the times" and operate accordingly.

Since it is so obvious that what Jesus established as his church does not in any way resemble the human organizational structures that now exist, thinking Catholics ponder the question: What kind of church did Jesus really intend to establish?

Faithful Catholics accept that we now have an institutional church with the Bishop of Rome at its head who has been given (by people, not by God) the title *Supreme Pontiff*. The pope holds what is referred to as the *Primacy*, with authority, power, and jurisdiction over the entire church. Together with finely delineated clerical structures, processes, and canon laws, the institutional church exercises what it considers Jesus to have empowered it to do when he said: "I will give you the keys of the kingdom of heaven, and whatever you bind on earth will be bound in heaven, and whatever you loose on earth will be loosed in heaven" (Matthew 16:19, *NRSV*).

Most of us Catholics love this church. We like having a home parish. We want to belong to a diocese or archdiocese. We respect our priests and bishops and cardinals and popes. We are proud of the universal nature of the church, the institutions we have built, the art we have made over the centuries. We honor and emulate our saints, including especially Mary, whom we call our "blessed mother."

But this does not mean we do not understand that the structures of the institutional church we have at the beginning of the third millennium of the

Christian movement are the only ones—or even the best ones—we can come up with. And we certainly don't have to believe that the institutional church we have now came directly and full-blown from Jesus himself.

Is that really what Tradition has taught us? Is that what Jesus taught his followers about his church? Or is there more to consider and to understand for those of us who want to be faithful to the teachings of the church and yet remain faithful to the truth of what Jesus really established, in totality, as his church?

I answer this last question with a resounding and faithful "yes." I am firmly convinced that the institutional church leaders have been deficient in addressing their own purpose and in the manner of their dialogue with the faithful. Their usual response to the faithful's queries on these organizational matters is greeted many times with a recitation of doctrines and principles they offer as justification for the "logic" of why the church is structured as it is today. But I do not accept that those of us are wrong who question and ask for a fuller understanding of the structure and operation of the church. In fact, I think that is what the faithful are supposed to be doing, because the *sensus fidei* (sense of the faith) and *sensus fidelium* (sense of the faithful) is the entire basis for the idea of Tradition, which the Catholic Church has always recognized as one of the two sources of divine revelation (the other, of course, being the Scriptures).

The word *developed* is of paramount importance to consider lest anyone imagines that it was Jesus who established the current organizational structures and practices on how to exercise authority in the church. An important insight on how the development of church practices and beliefs evolve was masterfully stated, not by some organizational sociologist but by Frederick Franck, a dental surgeon who worked for Albert Schweitzer in Africa. Franck was a painter and sculptor, a spiritualist, and the official artist of Vatican II. He said, "When logic follows experience, it is likely to be valid. When experience derives from logic, it is bound to be self-deception: delusional, spurious, false."

Even the most die-hard defender of the status quo inside the church would admit that Jesus certainly did not proclaim a set of governing by-laws to be followed in his church as a result of some logical extension of the accepted principles of organizational management of his time. The very idea is ludicrous.

Jesus' logic flowed, of course, from his being one with his Father. But he was also truly human, so he reflected on his experiences as he lived in the society of his times. For him to do it any other way would have meant that he was *not* truly human, at least in the way that we all are. So how did Jesus see things as *he* established the church *he* had in mind, the church that the "gates of hell" would never prevail against?

• • • • • •

Jesus experienced firsthand the complicity and hypocrisy of the religious hierarchs of the Temple.

• • • • • •

Jesus experienced firsthand the complicity and hypocrisy of the religious hierarchs of the Temple. Obviously, whether one prefers a conservative, moderate, or progressive reading of the New Testament, it is undeniable that Jesus, a faithful Jew, had no difficulty in seriously criticizing the religious leaders of his time. Jesus taught us that we could be faithful to our religious faith, yet we can also be (should also be?) questioning and constructively critical of both our church's leaders and of ourselves.

Most people who seriously reflect on the Gospels perceive that, whatever Jesus desired for his new church in about A.D. 30, he would be greatly surprised by its current stately organizational set-up, its regal image and the face of opulence that it presents to the world. (It seems that as of this writing Pope Francis is attempting to correct these impressions, but apparently not all the hierarchy or even all the laity are amenable.)

A good explanation of the nature of the church that Jesus desired as a result of what he experienced is contained in the fine theological reflection on the church in Capuchin Franciscan Michael H. Crosby's book, *Repair My House*. Also, there is (and I use here) the research of the many other fine theologians who have written about the establishment of Jesus' church in Matthew 16, when he named Peter as the "rock" upon which the church is built.

As with all theologizing, when we attempt to demonstrate how Scripture substantiates our position, it is essential that we not rely on just one, singular, "proof" text as unequivocal evidence presenting a total understanding for the truths of the faith. Jesus, we must always remember, is a divine mystery and his church is nothing less than a true reflection of that same divine mystery. Jesus' church is really a divine mystery and not just another human institution that can be understood with an organizational chart, a "chain of command," or a Code of Canon Law.

In Matthew 16:18-19 the evangelist relates that Jesus called Peter the "rock" upon which he will build his church and giving him the power to "bind" and "loose" on earth and promising that it will be done likewise in heaven. But we must remind ourselves not to fall into the trap of thinking we can fully understand Jesus' message by just citing one passage or incident of the Bible out of context. We must seek the full understanding of the mystery that Peter and the other disciples experienced. When we do this in regard to Peter and his relationship to the church, it helps to look for the same incident as it is related to us by other followers.

I invite you to refer to the other Gospel accounts that illuminate this passage in Matthew. It is remarkable that Mark (see Mark 8) and Luke (see Luke 9) make no mention whatsoever of Jesus saying to Peter that he is the "rock" upon which Jesus will build his church. Doesn't it strike you as quite strange that such an important and powerful indication as to Jesus' intentions about the church is not even mentioned by these two evangelists? I point this out not to say or even imply that therefore Jesus did not name Peter as the "rock" upon which his church was to be built. But I *am* saying that we must consider the other accounts regarding the founding of the church revealed in Scripture.

So, we must look further into Matthew's Gospel to see if he sheds an even brighter light on the truth about Peter's primacy in Jesus' church. In Matthew 18:18-20, when Jesus is talking to his disciples with Peter present, he says to the entire group:

> *"Truly I tell you, whatever you bind on earth will be bound in heaven, and whatever you loose on earth will be loosed in heaven. Again, truly I tell you, if two of you agree on earth about anything you ask, it will be done for you by my Father in heaven. For where two or three are gathered in my name, I am there among them"* (NRSV).

Jesus, now talking with *all* his disciples, gives the power to "bind" and "loose" to all those faithful assembled: "Truly I tell you, whatever you bind on earth will be bound in heaven, and whatever you loose on earth will be loosed in heaven." This is the same authority Jesus gave to Peter in Matthew 16. But in Matthew 18, Jesus now gives that same power to Jesus' followers. Many theologians cite this not in an attempt to negate the primacy of Peter and his successors but to present the context and full truth of how Jesus really established his church—a church in communion with all his followers.

With this fuller exposition, we can see that Jesus gave to Peter the "keys," i.e. authority, but when we reflect on Matthew 16:19 together with 18:18 we see the truth of that responsibility for authority in its totality. It is also given to the *community* of Jesus' followers (*ekklesia* in Greek). In essence, this fuller context demonstrates that Jesus established his church in which authority and power is not solely under the auspices of a clerical hierarchy (a clerical, ordained, institutionalized hierarchy) but are realized in the mystery of the communion of all Jesus' faithful followers—the "People of God" in the insightful phrase used by Vatican II to describe the entire church.

Indeed, Jesus established his church not as a structured human organization with office holders but as a communion of believers who under the inspiration and guidance of the Holy Spirit collegially share responsibility and authority. (What a wondrous mystery *that* is!)

In *The Message*, Eugene Peterson translates Matthew 18:18-20 this way:

"Take this most seriously: A yes on earth is yes in heaven; a no on earth is no in heaven. What you say to one another is eternal. I mean this. When two of you get together on anything at all on earth and make a prayer of it, my Father in heaven goes into action. And when two or three of you are together because of me, you can be sure that I'll be there."

This translation gives even further insight into the *nature* of the power and authority that the church is to exercise. It is more about authenticity and community than it is about rules and laws.

Jesus gives even further clarification about authority in his church and a warning as to the dangers of the misuse of power by those in authority. In Matthew 20:25-28 (*NRSV*) Jesus makes his experience forcefully clear: "You know that the rulers of the Gentiles lord it over them, and their great ones are tyrants over them. It will not be so among you; but whoever wishes to be great among you must be your servant, and whoever wishes to be first among you must be your slave; just as the Son of Man came not to be served but to serve, and to give his life a ransom for many."

Again, look at the translation of this passage from *The Message*:

You've observed how godless rulers throw their weight around, how quickly a little power goes to their heads. It's not going to be that way with you. Whoever wants to be great must become a servant. Whoever wants to be first among you must be your slave. That is what the Son of Man has done: He came to serve, not be served—and then to give away his life in exchange for the many who are held hostage."

With this poignant observation from Jesus, we are hit in the head with the truth as expressed by Frederick Franck: "When logic follows experience, it is likely to be valid. When experience derives from logic, it is bound to be self-deception: delusional, spurious, false." Jesus certainly was not delusional. He did not fall for the logic or hypocrisy of any one person or any authority—secular or religious. Indeed, we can appropriately use the contemporary expression about him: "He tells it like it is!"

To see this full context of Jesus' establishing his church on the "rock," Peter, it seems to me undeniable that Jesus gave to Peter *primacy* in his church, but it is *not* obvious to me that he was setting up a clerical-hierarchical church with Peter as its first dictator. It is confusing why many traditionalists are so fond of saying, "The church is not a democracy." Of course it is not a democracy; but neither is it a dictatorship. The church of Jesus Christ is the communion of faithful followers, all empowered to "bind" and "loose," but that is not to be confused with the operating dynamics of a human organizational entity. Whether one is carefully conservative or forcefully progressive, it is undeniable that Jesus was not seeking to establish anything close to the hypocritical legalisms of the Pharisees' governing model, which institutionalized a "clericalism" of powers.

The clericalism in the Catholic Church that has developed and evolved over these two thousand years is deeply rooted in the culture of too many in the hierarchy today. It is often the primary way they relate to rest of the People of God. This is a major stumbling block to understanding the church that Jesus imagined into existence. Jesus' church is not found in its institutional structures. Its reality lies in the communion of the People of God and the lived experience of *their* personal relationships with the Lord.

This observation could not have been more forcefully stated then it was at a March 22, 2014, address given in Rome at the Clementine Hall by Pope Francis to the Corallo Association:

You spoke of something else, which I mentioned in the Apostolic Exhortation Evangelii Gaudium. *You spoke about clericalism. It is one of the evils, one of the evils of the church. But it is a "complicit" evil, because priests take pleasure in the temptation to clericalize the laity, but many of the laity are on their knees asking to be clericalized, because it is more comfortable, it is more comfortable! This is a double sin! We must overcome this temptation. The layperson must be lay, one who is baptized, with the power that comes from his or her baptism.*

I believe that the institutional church has evolved with a clericalism as its *modus operandi,* one that runs counter to Jesus' vision for his church *and* counter to the attempted corrections made by Vatican II.

I dream of a church that can openly admit that the Holy Catholic Church is made up of laity and ordained who all admit we are sinners and imperfect. I dream of an institutional church that admits that it does not have all the answers to everything but with all its shortcomings, mistakes, and weaknesses has faith that the Holy Spirit will always inspire the People of God to read the signs of the times. I dream of a church that is not dictated to by a hierarchy but is persuasively led through a collegial communion of all the faithful by leaders who listen to and serve and treat all women and men equally in all things. I dream of a church that is inclusive of all, shows mercy and compassion to all, and serves all. I dream, therefore, of the church I believe Jesus had in mind: a church that flourishes because of its loving persuasion…not because of its imposed coercion.

CHAPTER 5

"Silence Is Golden,
But Sometimes It's Just Plain Yellow"

· · · · · ·

*If you're on the quest for the truth, you have to question things,
you have to question authority. That's the only way you can be
on a true quest for the truth. And so you have to end up speaking
truth to power.*

KERRY KENNEDY

· · · · · ·

No matter how many years we go back in the history of the church, we see struggles and challenges not only between leaders and their followers but also among institutional church leaders themselves. Even before Jesus ascended into heaven, the apostles (see Luke 22:24) quarreled with each other about who was greater. During the early times of the church, as more Gentiles converted to Christianity, disputes arose among the church leaders as to whether or not the Gentiles were required to conform to the Law of Moses. Even Paul observes (1 Corinthians 11:18): "For, to begin with, when you come together as a church, I hear that there are divisions among you; and to some extent I believe it." Or, as the same passage is translated in *The Message:* "I am getting the picture that when you meet together it brings out your worst side instead of your best! First, I get this report on your divisiveness, competing with and criticizing each other. I'm reluctant to believe it, but there it is."

We don't even have to go so far back in church history to see the divisions and arguments that have arisen. The most dramatic and divisive split in the church can be seen at the time of the Protestant Reformation, which came about primarily because of the devastating and corrupt culture deeply embedded within the medieval church's abuse of authority. Instead of the hierarchy attempting to be open and listen to many of the faithful voicing their criticism about the obvious abuses happening (many of which were finally admitted to and corrected by the church councils Vatican I and especially Vatican II), the church leaders instead became condemnatory of those who were making justified criticisms. Of course, there were also doctrinal issues that Martin Luther and others raised that should have been addressed. In fact, the Catholic and Lutheran Churches recently issued a joint statement on one of the most difficult, Luther's insistence that we are saved by faith alone, and were able to come to a joint statement on that issue. But let's be honest about it: There was very little hope of addressing those issues when the hierarchy would not even address the glaring abuses regarding the selling of salvation through indulgences, the ostentatious abuse of church wealth, and general institutional church corruption.

Imagine if the hierarchy at that time facilitated an honest and open dialogue with those who were calling for church reform. Imagine if the hierarchy admitted to the public their blatant transgressions and said, "We are wrong; we will change; we ask you for forgiveness." Would not that have been the Christian thing to do? Would not that have presented an opportunity for a possible transformation of church practices that may have avoided the Protestant schism that separates the western Christian community to this day?

But in today's church, with all the forces of disagreement, with the many public church scandals, with vast numbers (especially of our young adults) leaving the church, should we faithful Catholics just remain silent? Are we not to question or criticize our leaders to avoid another devastating schism (which I and co-author Sr. Cynthia Nienhaus, CSA, called "the silent schism" in our book of the same name? Is keeping silent in the church now our definition of being "a good Catholic"?

To seek insight into today's answers to the questions of fidelity, obedience, and orthodoxy, an historical perspective may be helpful. If we look back at the history of the Protestant Reformation, we find that the Catholic Church's response was to convene the Council of Trent (1545-1563). This Council was anything but open, compromising, or healing! It became quite obvious that the hierarchy was definitely not disposed to any *mea culpa* on their part, nor were they open to changing their ways or correcting their abuses. They just seemed, well, not to want to yield any of their power, perks, or practices. (Does this sound familiar to any of us today?)

Some have characterized the Council of Trent as the focal point at which the institutional church cemented its insidious bias toward hierarchical clericalism. Please understand my criticism of *clericalism* is not a criticism of *clerics* in any way. Clericalism is an attitude that any person may have—clergy or laity—that claims entitlement or superiority to those who are ordained to service by the church. The devastating nature of this culture was strikingly captured in the 2014 New Year's message of Archbishop Socrates Villegas of Lingayen-Dagupan, the Philippines, when he declared:

Clericalism speaks of privilege, prerogatives, entitlement, and special treatment. Clericalism prefers sacristies to the slums. Clericalism is more concerned with embroidered vestments than reconciled souls. When we look back at the history of the church, reform always started with clergy reform.

Am I exaggerating, misreading, or unfairly assessing the Council of Trent? Judge for yourself. At this Council there were 150 *anathemas* (i.e., denunciation, condemnation, and damnation) declared for anyone who did not acquiesce to what they, the clerical hierarchy of the time, declared to be the faith of the church. Yes, 150 times those who called out for transformation of institutional church abuses were damned. Do you believe the Council's proclamations and tone even remotely reflect the church that Jesus Christ founded? I don't. Think about it. One hundred and fifty times, reformers calling for corrective action were officially told to go to hell? Even if the bishops at the Council of

Trent were right on every issue (which they were not), was condemning those who disagreed with them a Christian response? No, it was not.

Though the 1983 Code of Canon Law finally did away with the "anathema" formula for excommunication, nevertheless it would be difficult to argue that vestiges of the Trentian culture do not still exist today in different ways. If you do not think that this is true, then how else would you assess how some current clashes have been addressed in recent institutional-church history?

For example, how would you characterize the treatment of theologians whose works are condemned behind surreptitious threats of reprisals without offering them an opportunity for open dialogue? What do you suppose is the feeling of lay Catholics who are denied access to the sacraments because their marriage failed, often through no fault of their own and after real attempts to save it? Can you imagine the distress of men and women who are told by the institutional church that because of their sexual orientation they are "disordered," even though science has made it clear, and they know from their own experience, that their sexuality is normal and natural and God-given? What about the many faithful Catholics, myself included, who believe women should be ordained into church service? Are we to accept being told to "shut up and do not even try to discuss this?"

My concern is whether the rest of us respond to these hurting people with the same Gospel values with which Jesus blessed his church.

Okay. Enough of that. My point is not to debate the legal and doctrinal elements of these situations, although I am willing and able to do so at the drop of a bishop's miter. Rather, my concern is whether the rest of us respond to these hurting people with the same Gospel values with which Jesus blessed his church.

Please do not misunderstand my message. I am not trying to diminish or disrespect the legitimate role of the pope, bishops, priests, and deacons within the institutional church. But I am insisting, without any recourse to ingratiating or obsequious formulations, that Jesus did not give his church ideological stones to throw at people; he gave us Peter, a "rock" that is to support, nourish, and care for all people with mercy and compassion. The Catholic Church cannot theologize, philosophize, nor canonize laws and rules as more important than to love every single person as Jesus loved us, that is, unconditionally. "Who am I to judge?" Pope Francis famously asked early in his papacy. Of course, non-judgmental love does not always make human sense. But it does make Christianity at its best! That's Christianity that the conservative, the moderate, and the progressive can and should all embrace. We must be "all things to all people."

I began this chapter with remarks by Kerry Kennedy, daughter of Robert Kennedy. I also share with you a further observation that she made when she presented the Keynote Address at the Call To Action Conference that took place in Memphis in 2014. She told about when, as a teenager, she attended one of the Vietnam War protest rallies. When she returned to school after that protest, instead of receiving criticism from the woman religious teaching her class, the woman said, "You know, Kerry, silence is golden, but sometimes it's just plain yellow." (As you see, I chose this as a fitting title of this chapter.) Without the *but* clause in the sister's observation, the whole truth and full impact of honest, free, and open dialogue is just a sham! Indeed, at times silence can be colored with a shade of cowardly yellow, even in the Catholic Church.

Anyone can see that the church, especially in the Western world, is losing its members to a frightening degree. In Europe attendance at Sunday Mass has dropped to under 15%. In the United States Sunday Mass participation went from 55% in 1965 to currently about 24%. And, if you look around in the pews, the scarcity of young adult faces is depressing. I do not understand how anyone, even the strictest interpreter of what it means to be Catholic, can see this exodus as something good and contributing to a stronger church.

Is that the Spirit of Jesus speaking to us today? Are we to be content with a church of exclusion of anyone who does not pass every single litmus test we can come up with? If this trend continues and the young no longer find Jesus in the Catholic Church, then what will the church look like in ten or twenty years and beyond?

We can no longer remain silent. Finding the courage to speak to authority and to one another respectfully and to openly seek solutions to our differences has risen to the stage of an obligatory requirement of faith. I am not saying that this obligation belongs exclusively to the lay people; it is imperative as well for the many dedicated and faithful vowed religious women and men, deacons, priests, bishops, cardinals, and popes who make up the entire People of God.

To equate docility with faithfulness is a sin. Even though Pope Francis is modeling to the hierarchy a transforming and open spirit, there is still resistance from many in positions of authority in the church. Much more work needs to be done to remedy this situation. The People of God have seen enough of those who have chosen to color with a yellow shade of golden silence.

In June 2014, we received a remarkable document entitled *Sensus Fidei in the Life of the Church* issued by the International Theological Commission. It is worth noting that this document was approved by Cardinal Gerhard Muller, Prefect of the Congregation of the Doctrine of the Faith. Also worth pointing out is that Pope Benedict XVI appointed the commission members before Francis became pope. These theologians were charged with explaining for today's church the meaning of the *sensus fidei* (individual believers' faith) and the *sensus fidelium* (the belief of the entire church).

The commission made it quite clear in this document that it is certainly not the curia and bishops in the church, isolated from all the People of God, who should define the deposit of faith for the believers. Quite clearly they state:

Putting faith into practice in the concrete reality of the existential situations in which he or she is placed by family, professional, and cultural relations enriches the personal experience of the believer. It enables him or her to see more precisely the value and the limits of a given doctrine, and to propose ways of refining its formulation. That is why those who teach in the name of the church should give full attention to the experience of believers, especially lay people, who strive to put the church's teaching into practice in the areas of their own specific experience and competence (59).

The commission made it clear that it was not saying that the deposit of faith is solely a matter of counting the popular vote of the majority: A further disposition necessary for authentic participation in the *sensus fidei* is attentiveness to the magisterium of the church and a willingness to listen to the teaching of the pastors of the church as an act of freedom and deeply held conviction (see 97). Perhaps, those of a more conservative persuasion will stress this passage in the Commission's report to underscore the role of the magisterium in regard to the Catholic faith.

Yet the commission certainly posits the importance and necessity of considering essential to the promulgation of any teaching the lived experience of all believers. But we cannot discern that lived experience if some, or many, or most of us are silenced because our church culture does not facilitate and encourage open and free dialogue. In fact the commission members further clarify their position when they state that "…sometimes the truth of the faith has been conserved not by the efforts of theologians or the teaching of the majority of bishops but in the hearts of believers" (119).

Throughout the thousands of years in which a creeping clericalism has infused itself within the culture of the institutional church, it is certainly refreshing to see an acknowledgement coming from an official Vatican Commission that all of us are an essential part of the true and full teaching communion of the church.

The culture within the institutional church has evolved over centuries into a well-choreographed ballet of dancers pirouetting around the stage presenting harmony and gracefulness, often while stabbing one another in the back. Most in the audience are no longer applauding this dance. It seems to me that Pope Francis is trying to introduce a much different dance style, but clearly all the dancers on the stage are not yet accepting the new choreography.

I dream of a church in which open and honest discussion takes place among the hierarchy as they listen to the lived experience of the faithful and where all women and men are truly integrated into the organization and authority structures of the church. I dream of a church that encourages clergy, vowed religious, lay women and men, and theologians of whatever school of thought to be free to seek the truth of the Gospel message in today's world without having to conform to the controls or limits imposed by the institutional church. I dream of the church of the People of God who are one in Christ, with all our diversity, doubts, and questions.

CHAPTER 6

Infallibility Is True, But It's Not Magic

• • • • • •

We shall find ourselves unable to fix an historical point at which the growth of doctrine ceased and the rule of faith was once and for all settled.

CARDINAL JOHN HENRY NEWMAN

• • • • • •

The First Vatican Council (1869-1870) convened by Pope Pius IX, which was the twentieth ecumenical council of the Catholic Church (Vatican II was the twenty-first), proclaimed the dogma on papal infallibility. Some are surprised that it took until the nineteenth century (and only after nineteen previous councils) before a dogma of such importance was formally declared. However, in different ways and with many nuances the traces of this claim of infallibility can be seen in how the church taught doctrine throughout its history.

Though the words *doctrine* and *dogma* are commonly used interchangeably, we should acknowledge a precise distinction. *Doctrine* is basically a "teaching" of the church, whereas a *dogma* is a doctrine that is explicitly taught as "infallible." In other words, just as all cognac is brandy but not all brandy is cognac, so too all dogma is doctrine but not all doctrine is dogma!

What follows is certainly a simplification of the dogma of papal infallibility, but it should suffice for our purposes. I like the following definition, gleaned from the decrees of Vatican Council I:

Papal infallibility is a divinely revealed dogma that gives to the pope the power to be without error when he exercises his office as "pastor" and "teacher" of all Christians, that is to say, in Latin, when he speaks ex cathedra. Furthermore, the pronouncement must be about a teaching on "faith" or "morals" and is to be held as true by the entire church and is "irreformable."

Also, it is enlightening for us today to recall the dynamics and tension that were strikingly present and intimately interwoven into the deliberations among the hierarchs who were part of Vatican Council I.

This grand body of clerics in no way could be described as coming together with a brotherly and harmonious embrace, eager to proclaim in unison and with complete accord the dogma of papal infallibility. There was in no way complete agreement with Pope Pius IX and his insistent drive to have this dogma declared. In fact, some theologians who have thoroughly researched and studied Vatican Council I are convinced that many of the attending bishops, even though they did want to strengthen papal authority, thought it a mistake to declare infallibility as a formal dogma of the church. In fact, some were so strongly opposed to such a formal declaration that, upon seeing that it would pass by a majority, fifty-seven participants walked out of the council before the vote took place. Unanimity was certainly not the hallmark of this dogma from its very inception.

There are voluminous theological writings, masterful expositions, and sophisticated explanations of what papal infallibility is and is not; when it should be applied and when it should not; how it should be declared and how it should not. Most of the clarifications and degrees of distinctions about how infallibility is exercised in the church involve mental gymnastics of Olympian proportions. In short, papal infallibility's implications for the faithful is anything but decided and undisputed.

But what are the practical implications of this dogma in today's church for those who want to be faithful to the teachings of the church in regards to papal infallibility and yet have questions, criticisms, and doubts in the way many of those in the institutional church understand and exercise that divine gift?

Indeed, today there is a gigantic quagmire of intricately and precisely crafted words, arguments, and explanations that only seem to be focused on rationalizing the unique power of the pope. There is very little discussion regarding its pastoral implications for the People of God. This becomes a glaring and significant phenomenon for today's faithful, who are respectfully seeking a more pertinent and practical understanding of this dogma and how it pertains to the faith decisions they must ultimately make *for themselves* in the sanctity of their own informed conscience and, ultimately, in their personal relationship to God.

Of course the faithful should make moral and faith decisions only after they seriously reflect on the church's teachings and dogmas. That is so obvious that it should not need to be stated. But stated it is, over and over again, by those who basically believe that there is only one conclusion that people can come to on a particular issue if they do so. That is, of course, absurd if you also believe in conscience, free will, and the sense of the faithful.

We followers of Jesus Christ and members of his church are morally, psychologically, and spiritually required to make decisions we must live with in our own lives as faithful Catholics. The hierarchy should no longer consider it reasonable, legitimate, or appropriate to coerce theologians, clergy, and laity into silence because they openly explore and question traditional church teachings. In fact, I believe we all have the obligation to ask and explore the difficult questions of faith and seek meaningful answers that speak to our times and relate to our understanding of diverse cultures in today's globalized societies.

Tradition and Scripture (the two sources of divine revelation according to the Catholic Church) are both clear that the Holy Spirit inspires all the faithful followers of Jesus and not just institutional church office holders. In his book, *Moral Theology: A Continuing Journey*, Charles E. Curran reflected that, "There can be no absolute division between the hierarchy as the teaching church and the rest of the faithful as the learning church." Theologians and any of the faithful who openly and honestly question doctrine should not be labeled as dissenters. A more just and Christian attitude, especially from the institutional church leaders, should consider them faithful seekers of truth. (In my book, *Flying in the Face of Tradition: Listening to the Lived Experience of the Faithful*, I explore this idea at more length.)

Of course, some church leaders insist that they are only trying to protect the faithful from confusion when they defend the magisterium (the body of church teachings). But it is church authority's imposition of forced silence, its prohibition of questions, and its threats of disciplinary actions on theologians and others that elicit confusion among the faithful. Openness, dialogue, and "faith seeking understanding" is not confusion. It's the Catholic intellectual tradition going all the way back at least to Thomas Aquinas—if not to Paul. I have some hope that Pope Francis, who is encouraging such thinking, will be able to turn the Roman Curia and the bishops around on this issue, given enough time.

• • • • • •

Without both divine gifts of revelation at work, papal infallibility would not reflect the basic truth of the communion that Jesus proclaimed for his church.

• • • • • •

I am quite sure that Pope Francis agrees that infallibility is not something that occurs at a particular moment when the Holy Spirit infuses into the head of a pope a dogma that emerges as an eternally true statement from his lips. It is only a coercive and restrictive attitude on the part of a few that makes a mockery of the gift of infallibility in the church. Infallibility is a gift of the Holy Spirit to the entire church that occurs only in the (very) rare and solemn instances when the pope proclaims a truth about faith or morals to the faithful People of God after discerning and listening to the faithful's lived experience of following Jesus Christ. To do this, the pope needs *both* the divine gift of the Holy Spirit and the divine gift of the human experience inspired by the Holy Spirit within the People of God. Without both divine gifts of revelation at work, papal infallibility would not reflect the basic truth of the communion that Jesus proclaimed for his church.

Bluntly speaking, papal infallibility is not magic. This is what needs to be said, and I am saying it now. We faithful have questions and seek clarifications regarding the dogma on infallibility. We readily see the common sense obligation for the institutional church's unequivocal spiritual duty to seek guidance from the Holy Spirit, but we also know that the hierarchy must continuously learn and listen to the lived experience of all the faithful as the Holy Spirit inspires us. Furthermore, we realize that the institutional church has the common sense obligation to incorporate the evolving new knowledge discovered in psychology, medicine, societal dynamics, cultural diversity, human sexuality, etc., into official church teaching—even if it means we have to change some of our teachings and practices. (The joke going around Rome is that whenever the church does change something, it always starts by proclaiming "As we have always taught…." That is fine with me, as long as they change.)

Reading the signs of the times has always been the spiritual grace given by the Holy Spirit to the entire People of God. It is what allows us to be reliable and relevant proclaimers of the Gospel. It is what allows all of us to evangelize. That is still true for the third millennium, whether some in church leadership like it or not.

Those who question and seek to understand the meaning and usefulness of the dogma of infallibility should not be considered by anyone, especially by those in authority, as persons who are disloyal to the church or who lack faith. Rather, it may well be that faithful questioning people have a more realistic and accurate understanding of the infallibility of the church than those who unquestioningly adhere to a formulaic presentation of this mystery. That is why Cardinal Newman's insight opening this chapter is so relevant: "We shall find ourselves unable to fix an historical point at which the growth of doctrine ceased and the rule of faith was once and for all settled."

No, papal infallibility is not magic. On the contrary, it is we the faithful, taking our faith seriously, confronting our doubts, and seeking to make sense of the lives we are living in this world, who are infallible—not individually but collectively with the pope and the magisterium, solemnly proclaimed, and over a very long period of time. The pope articulates what God has revealed through the faithful's lived experience. For example, it is essential, realistic, and absolutely necessary for the pope to speak clearly using the most current knowledge available to all humans through the advancements in information technology, in the sciences, and in basic human, sexual, and spiritual development. Historical explanations of dogma and doctrines that were once meaningful to the People of God in the past may not always be relevant or appropriate for those of us in today's world.

In essence, what I am saying is that the dogma of infallibility should not preclude new knowledge or new insights being unfolded and discovered. What lies at the infallible core of any particular truth is God's unconditional and unlimited love! How could it possibly be otherwise?

It should be observed that even though no formal, authoritative list of infallible *ex cathedra* dogmas has ever been published by the Vatican, it appears that there are only three dogmas that have been solemnly declared infallible teachings. First is the actual dogma itself on infallibility, decreed by Vatican I. Second is the doctrine of Mary's Immaculate Conception, declared by Pope Pius IX in 1854 and incorporated as an infallible teaching after Vatican I in 1870. Pope Pius XII declared the third dogma in 1950: Mary's bodily Assumption into heaven.

Every official teaching of the magisterium or the pope himself or official written documents do not necessarily satisfy the criteria for a specifically, solemnly proclaimed, and *ex cathedra* binding belief for all the faithful. There are some Catholics, however, who consider ordinary teachings as binding, definitive, and irreformable. A glaring example of this controversy is the 1994 Apostolic Letter, *Ordinatio Saccerdotalis,* in which Pope John Paul II stated:

"I declare that the church has no authority whatsoever to confer priestly ordination on women and that this judgment is to be definitively held by all the church's faithful (4).

Here you see the problem. There is absolutely no universal agreement among theologians or even among the clergy and the hierarchy as to the infallibility of this statement, since it is not obvious that this statement meets the criteria for being a solemn and clear proclamation manifesting itself to be *ex cathedra*. Many, many good Catholics do not think so, so how could even the pope possibly pronounce it as a dogma, much less a closed question. That would truly be flying in the face of Tradition!

All I am doing is scratching the surface on the topic of infallibility. There are many professional, faith-filled, and dedicated theologians who have researched this and other topics and still have serious questions that seem to be endless and quite intriguing. (If you want to do a serious study of how church teaching changes over the years, look into the question of *usury*, which the church at one time considered to be a serious sin and now ignores almost completely.)

An example and a glimpse of some creative theological reflection on the dogma of infallibility can be seen in a presentation given at the Catholic Theological Society of America's annual convention held in Miami, Florida, in 2008. Here, Margaret O'Gara (1947-2012), outgoing President of CTSA, observed: "Rather than appearing as an unchanging grasp of the truth, infallibility could be reinterpreted as the process through which, over time, the church discerns core teachings of the gospel for its age and culture." If the institutional church explored such a timely insight, given the vast explosion of new scientific knowledge discovered recently, perhaps O'Gara's theological reflection could assist the church to a more profoundly Christian and acceptable understanding of the dogma on infallibility.

Those interested in pursuing this topic more thoroughly should study the creative theological research and exploration on infallibility by the insightful theologian, Charles E. Curran. Among his many poignant observations, Curran sees difficulty for the magisterium to proclaim dogmas as infallible if they are derived from a reading of the Natural Law, since those "truths" are not derived from Scripture. What we know for sure is that Natural Law evolves over time as new scientific discoveries are made. In fact, Curran points out that when, as a priest in the early 1970s, Cardinal William Levada, former Prefect of the Congregation of the Doctrine of the Faith, wrote his doctoral dissertation at the Pontifical Gregorian University in Rome, he addressed this topic. Levada contended that the Natural Law by its very nature does not depend primarily on the Bible but evolves within the process of human reason and is thereby subject to change as new scientific knowledge is discovered.

Just to complicate (Oh, I mean clarify!) matters more, the application of the dogma of infallibility pertaining to the church's magisterium is enunciated in the 1983 Code of Canon Law (750-1):

> *A person must believe with divine and Catholic faith all those things contained in the word of God, written or handed on, that is in the one deposit of faith entrusted to the church, and at the same time proposed as divinely revealed either by the solemn magisterium of the church or by its ordinary and universal magisterium* **which is manifested by the common adherence of the Christian faithful** *under the leadership of the sacred magisterium; therefore all are bound to avoid any doctrines whatsoever contrary to them." (Emphasis supplied.)*

With this extremely important qualification, "which is manifested by the common adherence of the Christian faithful," we are brought to see a tremendously efficacious role that the institutional church acknowledges for the faithful when it come to the dogma of infallibility. However, do any of us faithful hear about this when someone proclaims a specific teaching to be definitive? Or, do we somehow just get one message: You must believe this as "definitive" without further questioning because it is a "definitive teaching" that must not be questioned.

With this "common adherence" qualification in Canon Law, some theologians and many of the faithful believe that church teachings must be open to dialogue, questioning, and *adherence* by the faithful. In fact, some say, with reasonable justification, that a particular teaching may not be infallible in the first place if *"common adherence of the Christian faithful"* is not present. Again, why is it that the hierarchy does not discuss this article of Canon Law with the faithful?

The aim of this chapter is merely to give a brief context of the vast topic on the church and infallibility. I only seek to point out the questions and difficulties that are present in the common understanding of infallibility.

But I do dream of a future church in which infallibility is not confused by anyone as a "magic whisper" from the Holy Spirit into the ear of a pope or into the ears of bishops informing them about truth. I dream of a church that never fears that scientific discoveries could ever contradict any of what is true about God's creation. And, when some scientific knowledge does prove to contradict a fact that the church thought was true, I trust the church will have the humility and faith to accept the truth. I believe in a church that is smart enough to speak infallibly of God's unconditional love and not dumb enough to proclaim any dogmas or doctrines that intend to exclude or control that love in words, laws, and rules that we insist are definitive for everyone and for all time.

CHAPTER 7

Certainty Is Good, But to Doubt Is Human

• • • • • •

Doubt thou the stars are fire,
Doubt that the sun doth move.
Doubt truth to be a liar,
But never doubt I love.

WILLIAM SHAKESPEARE

• • • • • •

Over the two-thousand-year development of the structures and culture of the Catholic Church, an aura of certainty in what and how it teaches has solidified in many people's perception. Now, certitude is certainly a good thing in many ways. It is good that we know that God loves us unconditionally, for example. But it is equally true that no one—not even the pope—always knows the mind of God on every single issue of faith or morals. This truth is so self-evident that it should need no debate. But apparently it does.

Specifically, the behavior of the ordained, unmarried men who run the institutional church has not been immune from these dynamics. Certitude has infused their *modus operandi,* whether intentionally or by osmosis. For some of the faithful, this kind of spiritual attitude gives comfort and stability to their existence and lets them know they are doing God's will if they simply follow the institutional church's directives. For those receptive to this type of spiritual certainty, doubts are eradicated and psychological comfort is achieved without the tensions caused by uncertainty and ambiguity.

The only problem with this approach is that it does not appear to be what

Jesus had in mind. In fact, any fair reading of the Gospels would conclude that a well-established group of religious leaders at his time were sure that they were right, that they knew the mind of God, and that if people just followed their rules they could be assured that they were justified. It can be argued that a large part of Jesus' message and the reason that these religious leaders called for Jesus' death was that he was rejecting this very view of certainty and replacing it with a simple rule of "do the loving thing."

There are too many examples of this to cite here, but the story of the Pharisee and the sinner praying in the temple clearly summarizes Jesus' view:

> He also told this parable to some who trusted in themselves that they were righteous and regarded others with contempt: "Two men went up to the temple to pray, one a Pharisee and the other a tax collector. The Pharisee, standing by himself, was praying thus, 'God, I thank you that I am not like other people: thieves, rogues, adulterers, or even like this tax collector. I fast twice a week; I give a tenth of all my income.' But the tax collector, standing far off, would not even look up to heaven, but was beating his breast and saying, 'God, be merciful to me, a sinner!' I tell you, this man went down to his home justified rather than the other; for all who exalt themselves will be humbled, but all who humble themselves will be exalted."
>
> Luke 18:14-19, *NRSV*

Note the big "but" in the middle of Jesus' parable. Eugene Peterson translates verse 19 in *The Message* this way: "Jesus commented, 'This tax man, not the other, went home made right with God. If you walk around with your nose in the air, you're going to end up flat on your face, but if you're content to be simply yourself, you will become more than yourself.'"

So much for certainty. In fact, Jesus was totally frustrated with religious leaders who thought they knew it all. At one point he told them: "Truly I tell you, the tax collectors and the prostitutes are going into the kingdom of God ahead of you" (*NRSV*).

Given what may be reasonably described as Pope Francis' introduction of a less rigid, less controlling, and more pastoral spirit in the functioning of the Catholic Church, some fear a significant diminishment of that comforting spiritual certainty that became the hallmark in the church's historical workings. The introduction of doubt where certainty has always reigned is viewed as dangerous for the faithful adherents of Catholicism. This is absurdity!

Pope Francis sees a Catholic Church that will transcend the traditional and more rigid certainty of doctrinal and regulatory approaches. As I pointed out previously, he sees the real church as a messy church that welcomes all: believers and non-believers, the orthodox and the seekers, women as well as men, heterosexuals and those with other sexual orientations, and even those of us who are doubters regarding certainty itself.

Many are fearful that a more open and even more doubting church will cause a collapse in what I have come to call the Church of Certainty, but perhaps such a collapse of the institutional church will prove to be a blessing for the church. Is such a collapse of a church without doubts something to fear, or is it something that follows true—and traditional—Gospel values?

I was always puzzled, as a Catholic high school student and again while attending a Catholic university, when we studied a particular passage describing the Passion of Christ on the Cross:

And about three o'clock Jesus cried with a loud voice, "Eli, Eli, lema sabachthani?" that is, "My God, my God, why have you forsaken me?"
Matthew 27:46, *NRSV*

My bewilderment was persistent even after explanations by many fine teachers. The nagging conundrum haunting my mind for years was that this doubt on the part of Jesus was inexplicable, even after the professors' attempts at explanations. How could it be that the Divine Son of God and Second Person of the Holy Trinity, at the culmination of his saving act for all humanity, could express doubt that the God whom he called "Father" was with him, even at such a horrible time.

Yes, I learned that Jesus' cry on the cross was a quotation from the messianic psalm (Psalm 22) where the brutality and agony the "suffering servant" would experience is foretold. And I do realize that the Psalm goes on to give a very optimistic view of the future, even though Jesus never got to finish reciting it. Even with all the learned research I received from so many gifted theologians and biblical scholars, however, it is still difficult for me to understand in what sense Jesus was "forsaken" by his Father.

Yet over my own lifetime I have had many experiences in which I felt abandoned by God and began to doubt if there were any value in my suffering or in the suffering that I caused others. As I read, heard, and contemplated the many different theological insights into the doubt-plagued phenomenon that Jesus experienced on the cross, I not only came to accept my own doubts but those very doubts led me to better understand the growing and flourishing faith given to me by God. I began to appreciate that Jesus was not God pretending to be human. After all, if Jesus was not truly human, how could he know what we humans have to live through? He had to experience for himself the pain, hunger, sickness, meanness, sin, terror, and horrors in this world. Oh yes, there are many pious sounding exhortations and learned discourses given to us about suffering, but of those explanations none of them really eradicates the lingering doubt about the spiritual meaning of it all.

I believe Pope Francis gave a powerful, meaningful, and compelling faith-filled explanation (not a rationalized, dogmatized, indoctrinated, or otherwise intellectualized one) in his response to a tearfully-sobbing twelve-year-old girl, Glyzelle Palomar. She grew up in abject poverty by feeding herself from garbage dumps and never had a home to live in. She asked the pope in front of over 30,000 at a gathering of young people on his 2015 visit to the Philippines, "Why did God let this happen to us?" Pope Francis, putting aside his prepared presentation, answered with great wisdom. Following are some comments selected from his extemporaneous reply:

- "The nucleus of your question almost doesn't have a reply."
- "Only when we too can cry about the things that you said are we able to come close to replying to that question."
- "Why do children suffer so much?"
- "Certain realties in life we only see through eyes that are cleansed through our tears."

I believe Jesus was truly divine, with all the attributes of omnipotence. But what I now see more clearly is that when he was on the cross he showed his true humanity. Jesus doubted, as all humans do, precisely because he was truly human. Yet he also had faith in God. In the Garden of Gethsemane he prayed: "Not my will, but yours be done." (Luke 22:42, *NRSV*).

As the father with the mute son said to Jesus, "I believe; help my unbelief!" (Mark 9:24, *NRSV*). What I take from this is that without doubts faith has no real place in people's spiritual lives. Henry David Thoreau expressed a similar thought when he wrote: "Faith keeps many doubts in her pay. If I could not doubt, I should not believe."

I believe the proper conclusion the church should draw is obvious. Tradition should inform us that Jesus, a real human person, founded his church in spite of his human doubts because he possessed a divine gift of faith. Jesus, in his humanity, did not possess verifiable certitude that he lived his life and accepted his death responding to his Father's callings. But he did have unwavering faith that he was doing the will of his heavenly Father by teaching and acting completely out of love. Thus, Jesus' true human-divine nature is a mystery and can only be approached within the realm of human doubt.

> • • • • • •
>
> *Jesus, in his humanity, did not possess verifiable certitude...but he did have unwavering faith that he was doing the will of his heavenly Father by teaching and acting completely out of love.*
>
> • • • • • •

In his divine wisdom, the Son of God gave the Holy Spirit to the entire People of God, his church, to inspire and guide us despite the doubts that are an unavoidable part of the human condition. So I find it contrary to Tradition when the institutional church or any of its hierarchy convey the sense that they have no doubts about the words they speak and write. There seems to be an excessive and unreasonable fear on the part of some of our leaders that the floodgates would be wide open about all its teachings if they ever admit that an historical doctrine should be updated or redefined because current knowledge indicates the former teaching is inadequate or no longer convincing. This persistent refusal by the institutional church to revisit past teachings even when science and new insights are discovered is probably the single most important reason why many faithful Catholics, especially young people, are leaving the Catholic Church in droves.

People see clearly that with the advancement of knowledge no person or entity, especially the institutional church, can ignore the truth for fear of admitting a new awareness has modified an understanding of an old belief. Every day throughout the history of the world people discover something new about the world and about the people that God created. It is inconceivable that the institutional church leaders who believe in God's Creation could ever fear that some new scientific truth or insight into peoples lived realities and the material world could be against Natural Law or God's design.

An insightful theologian, Sister Margaret Farley, in her essay, "Ecclesiology, Ethics and the Grace of Self-Doubt," has explained this idea beautifully:

> *One of the least recognized gifts of the Spirit, however, may be what I call the "grace of self-doubt." If all co-believers are to participate in moral discernment in the church, and if the limited contribution of each requires the participation of the others, then all—laity, clergy, theologians, church leaders—have need of the grace of self-doubt.*

Farley goes on to explain that this "grace of self-doubt" is never doubt about the basic, profound, and core truth of God's love for all of us and the inestimable dignity of all human life. That alone is the rock on which the church was and should be built.

Problems occur when there is no doubt on anyone's part that past beliefs cannot be understood differently or modified when new knowledge is discovered that belies an older understanding. The church is best served when its leaders are humble and open enough to know that God's Creation is so magnificent, expansive, and awesome that its secrets are unlocked to humanity over time. The People of God, who are assured that the Holy Spirit's presence is among them, should never fear to doubt things from the past if they make them more receptive to God's revelations for the here-and-now.

Think about some current issues facing the church:

- Today, institutional church leaders do not seem to doubt that the moral objections to the use of artificial birth control they promulgated and still defend is valid and may never be changed. The overwhelming majority of married, faithful Catholics, in fact, practice artificial birth control and see no moral problem with this. Should not the hierarchy at least consider whether they might not see and fully understand God's gift of human sexuality, lovingly and intimately expressed between two people? Should not these same men listen to and engage with the many fine theologians and persons in intimate loving relationships who are asking for reconsideration of the institutional church's teachings on human sexuality? How can they ignore the results of credible research and study of the latest scientific, social, and theological insights? Why are they instead trying to silence voices of doubt?

- Today, institutional church leaders still do not seem to doubt that they have a full and correct understanding of the role of women in the church. They proclaim many gracious, pious, and laudatory accolades about women. However, they still permit some bishops or pastors to exclude female altar servers in their churches or diocese, arguing that it feminizes a role that is needed to attract boys to the all-male priesthood. The hierarchy (and so far the pope) does not permit women to be ordained as deacons, even though many fine theologians (and especially the research and study on this topic by Phyllis Zagano) have demonstrated that historically the church, in fact, did ordain women to the diaconate. They not only do not permit women to be ordained to the ministerial priesthood, in fact they say we are not even allowed to talk about it! Yet again many fine theologians have solid insights that clearly demonstrate gender is not a criterion that should be used on the issue of ordination to the priesthood.

- Today, institutional church leaders still seem to think there is no need to discuss their description of people who are LGBT as "disordered" and their expression of sexual intimacy as morally and gravely evil. They seem to have no doubt that they may in fact be contributing to the unchristian denigration of so many people. Science is more and more convincingly demonstrating that attraction to same sex relationships are not a matter of choice but of genetics. In other words, God made gay, lesbian, bi-sexual, and transgender people the way they are, just like God made heterosexuals the way they are.

Of course this list could go on for many more pages, including a long analysis of the causes of pedophilia and its subsequent cover-up in the church. The important message in all of this is that the church cannot be relevant or credible in the world if it is not willing to discuss its past teachings and behavior when credible new knowledge is introduced that makes it necessary to respond to the truth in God's Creation. It is *not* a sign of weakness to modify or change a past belief, but it *is* a sign of Christian faith to listen to the God who is continually revealing his truth to women and men gifted with the same Holy Spirit that Jesus blessed us with over two thousand years ago.

I dream of a church where doubts are always present, with one exception: that the church never doubts that God loves all of us unconditionally. I dream of a church that does not make judgments about how and who people love in a mutual, respectful, and freely chosen relationship. I dream of a church that, from the pope to those in the pews, can openly and freely express their doubts without being accused of disloyalty. I dream of a church where we can say with Christian faith, *"I believe; help my unbelief."*

CHAPTER 8

It's "Change," But Is It "Transformation"?

· · · · · ·

Change fixes the past. Transformation creates the future.

THE PRIMES (theprimes.com)

· · · · · ·

Simply stated, we contemporary Catholics are not coming together in any manner that anyone could say reflects Jesus' prayer, *"that we may all be one"* (John 17:21, *NRSV*). This is the reality in today's Catholic Church.

Of course, depending on our views, understanding, and beliefs about what the church is and how it should operate, we must all decide what is needed to remedy our discord or we will fly apart. Complicating matters is the fact that the Catholic Church is not a secular organization but a spiritual reality. As we pray in the Creed at Mass, we want to make it "one," "holy," "catholic" (in the sense of universal and for everyone), and "apostolic" (that is, in a straight line with the original disciples of Jesus). This is no small task, and without the guidance of the Holy Spirit we could not even contemplate it. But try we must, for the good of the kingdom of God that is to come "on earth, as it is in heaven." This was Jesus' big idea and is the mission on which we have all been sent— conservatives, moderates, and progressives alike—at the end of each and every Mass, by virtue of our baptism and confirmation.

In order to accomplish this mission, however, we must do two things at once. We must "all be one" and we must also and at the very same time "be all things to all people." It is a conundrum approaching an oxymoron, but there it is. And to accomplish it, we must transform our church, not just change it.

But how can we possibly accomplish this noble quest for communion and unity on the one hand and openness and inclusivity on the other? Is there a way to integrate the church's reality as a divine mystery with its concurrent human organizational dynamics? How do we overcome the current impasse that is preventing the much-needed healing in our church?

The first and foundational premise that is probably the most difficult to embrace as we begin this quest for healing is to understand and then agree on the following: Our church does not need *change*; it needs *transformation*. Though in ordinary conversation these two terms are often used interchangeably, they are certainly not the same. This is not merely an inconsequential matter of semantics. We as the People of God need to come to grips with these two distinct concepts, since these two approaches are quantitatively and qualitatively different.

To change, as it applies to the church, has come to imply the ability to fix established organizational structures in order to make them better. In other words, to change things means that the church will be what it has always been and it will do what it has always been doing, but in a (much) better way. In other words, the basic nature and culture of the church is not transformed—only some of its structures and operations change. Changing the church is what we have been trying to do since Vatican II; but what many believe is that Saint Pope John XXIII set out to transform the church.

To transform, as it applies to the church, is something quite different. The task for the church to transform itself is much more challenging and more difficult than simply fixing it, and it may be impossible to get all our members to buy in. To transform the church means to create a "future church" that basically infuses new ideas, new culture, and new structures into the entire People of God, and in essence it creates a new (transformed) church with entirely new dynamics. As leadership consultant Jim Sniechowski, Ph.D., points out:

Once you are transformed you are not and can never be what you once were. You have changed to the depth of your identity. It's not a change regarding this or that about you. You have changed. You are a different person and the change is through and through.

Not surprisingly, and humanly speaking, most leaders in any organization do not react favorably when threats to their power, status, and perks of office are attempted. True transformation of any institution is not usually undertaken, led, supported, or even accepted by the current custodians of the organization. This resistance commonly has nothing to do with the clear, objective, and obvious necessity to create a new vision for a group or, in this case, a church that is in turmoil and losing members. So the first and most difficult hurdle that we as church encounter today is that we cannot look to the top for transformation. We must lead the transformation ourselves.

As I work in the church, as I worship in the church, as I belong to a religious order within the church, as I remain a committed member of the church, I am constantly struggling with my conviction that transformation, not just change, is absolutely and urgently needed in the Catholic Church.

Now, I am certainly encouraged, joy-filled, and hope-filled over the magnificent and Christ-like spirit that Pope Francis has brought to the church since the beginning of his pontificate. I am in awe of his courage and determination to concretely effect changes in the institutional church through the committees and reforms that he has initiated to address current church organizational dynamics. I support and pray that he continues and perseveres in these initiatives. But despite my great respect for and support of and faith in Pope Francis, I must honestly observe that as of now (this book is being written in early 2016) I see only change being facilitated, not transformation.

I make this judgment without any diminishment in my loyalty to Pope Francis' efforts to bring compassion, mercy, and sensitivity to the entire church. I am realistic enough to surmise that the pope is pragmatic enough to start with changes in structures and in the pastoral tone of the church's way of doing business that will set the stage for a future transformation. Yet I believe that it is critical for us to see the distinction.

We will not always have Francis with us and—even if his successor embraces his vision for the church—we and the Holy Spirit are going to have a fight on our hands if we want real transformation of the church. Given the reality of the recent sex and financial scandals, their cover-ups, and the resurgence of clericalism, it becomes a necessity for the rest of the People of God to insist on a complete transformation of the church. It is only through a faith-filled response to the Holy Spirit's fervor that unity can become a reality. We can no longer accept what an increasing number of the faithful see as the nakedness of some of the institutional church leader's hypocrisy in dealing with their own (admitted, in some cases) internal shortcomings and their embarrassingly exclusionary and judgmental dictums against people with contrary views. Of course none of us knows if Pope Francis' efforts will result in the needed transformation, and we must support him at all costs. But we cannot settle for superficial changes.

• • • • • •

We can no longer accept what an increasing number of the faithful see as the nakedness of some of the institutional church leader's hypocrisy.

• • • • • •

Candidly, if any of us think that shuffling around various Vatican and diocesan personnel while adding some lay people and a sprinkling of women in select positions are all that is needed in the church, we are seriously misreading the signs of the times. Yes, such change is helpful and should be applauded, but it is not what is needed to take the church into the twenty-first century. That transformation will not happen if the faithful remain docile and silent. We need many dedicated and well-intentioned cardinals, bishops, priests, religious sisters and brothers, and especially lay people to witness, by their words and especially by their magnificent service to human-kind, what it means to be a church that seriously follows Jesus' Gospel. It is they who are the ones, in fact, who are beginning to lead the way to the transformation needed in the church.

Far too many of us remain silent because we rightfully fear that our criticism will be viewed as disloyalty to the church we lovingly serve. There are many who do not speak out because they fear institutional church recriminations against them, based on the threats and firings and excommunication we have all witnessed. That is why the more courageous among us, whether on the altar or in the pews, must start to speak out publicly, assertively, and faithfully in support of the new tone and direction set by Pope Francis. Transformation in the church will happen only if we demand it.

In this regard, I am not referring only to the human organizational dynamics that institutions should heed in order to be relevant to the inevitable societal evolution that is always present. Rather, the People of God must be more attuned and sensitive to the spiritual mandate for transformation conveyed by the apostle Paul when he said in unequivocal terms:

> *Do not be conformed to this world, but be transformed by the renewing of your minds, so that you may discern what is the will of God—what is good and acceptable and perfect.*
>
> Romans 2:2, NRSV

Paul tells us so clearly that the spiritual mission and duty which is at the core of how we are to be a church demands that the faithful "not be conformed to this world" but rather that our obligation is to renew our minds. Eugene Peterson's translation in *The Message*, puts the same verse from Romans this way:

> *Don't become so well-adjusted to your culture that you fit into it without even thinking. Instead, fix your attention on God. You'll be changed from the inside out. Readily recognize what God wants from you, and quickly respond to it. Unlike the culture around you, always dragging you down to its level of immaturity, God brings the best out of you, develops well-formed maturity in you.*

If our mission as church is to help God's kingdom come on earth, as it is in heaven, we will need an imagination that follows the inspiration of the Holy Spirit to substantially transform people's vision of the church. Nothing less will be enough. To be the People of God is to be Christians who are transforming the very core of our lives together in a church that is not merely content with tweaking structural mechanisms. To be the People of God means to respond to the Holy Spirit in today's world.

It is necessary for us to understand the dynamics of what the conflict is inside the church and the dissonance the faithful must live with as we approach a solution. Let me briefly explain what I believe to be the context of our current dilemma.

Hans Kung beautifully and powerfully unfolded the core soul of being a church in a most compelling context when he wrote in his famous book, *Does God Exist?*:

> *I can trust in faith that the spirit of God is not an enslaving spirit, that he is no other than the Spirit of the one taken up to God, the Spirit of Jesus Christ. And since Jesus is the one taken up to God, he is in the Spirit the living Lord, the standard for both the individual Christian and the ecclesial community. In light of this concrete standard, I can also test and discern the spirits. No hierarchy, no theology, no fanaticism seeking to invoke the "Spirit," without regard to Jesus, to his word, to his behavior, and to his fate can in fact lay claim to the Spirit of Jesus Christ. Here, then, any obedience, any agreement, any participation reaches its limits.*

Kung gives us a context for the People of God that does not support any attempt to duplicate some past nostalgic institution in which clerical authority was unchallenged and its control was absolute. As if that were ever really the case! The essence of the Catholic Church is to take seriously Jesus' continuous challenge to the rich young man (and to all of us) to simply "Come, follow me" (Mark 10:21, *NRSV*). This is not a formula for control by any hierarchy or for over-reliance on any code or canons of laws and regulations. As Kung insists: "No hierarchy, no theology, no fanaticism seeking to invoke the 'Spirit' without regard to Jesus, to his word, to his behavior, and to his fate can in fact lay claim to the Spirit of Jesus Christ."

The context for transformation of the Catholic Church should be judged not only as some ready-made doctrinal or organizational changes that, indeed, must and will be made. Rather, transformation begins when the faithful see an emerging vision of a church in which equality and mutuality of all the faithful can coexist as one in unity with the Holy Spirit. We must see an institutional church that understands and operates as it serves the church by being responsible and accountable to all the People of God.

We do have different ministries in the church, but not different holiness. Clergy are part of the reality that is the People of God just as vowed religious sisters and brothers and the laity are. Clericalism is an attitude, a set of behaviors, an institutional culture that fosters power, privileges, domination, exclusion of women, and a special status of holiness to select individuals. We need to understand that clericalism is not just a distorted trait of some in the ordained clergy but an attitude that can be a temptation to anyone who exercises leadership in the church.

Vatican II attempted to shatter clericalism. It tried to sever the church from its nostalgic past and substitute the model of the church as a People of God who are equals. Of course, in that communion of the faithful there will always be different and diverse responsibilities and functions that must be performed. Different and diverse, yes! Superior and inferior, no. Never!

In *Lumen Gentium* (*Light of the Nations*), the Dogmatic Constitution on the Church promulgated in 1964 by Pope Paul VI, the importance of the sacred teaching authority of the formal magisterium of the church is made very clear.

But what is often not stressed and seems not to be highlighted by many in the hierarchy to this day (and I wonder why not?) is the context in which the document speaks of the teaching authority of the church. Clearly it presents a new understanding of collegiality:

> *The holy people of God shares also in Christ's prophetic office; it spreads abroad a living witness to him, especially by means of a life of faith and charity and by offering to God a sacrifice of praise, the tribute of lips that give praise to his name. The entire body of the faithful, anointed as they are by the Holy One, cannot err in matters of belief. They manifest this special property by means of the whole people's supernatural discernment in matters of faith when "from the bishops down to the last of the lay faithful" they show universal agreement in matters of faith and morals. That discernment in matters of faith is aroused and sustained by the Spirit of truth.*
>
> Chapter II, "On the People of God," 12

Admittedly, there are many in the institutional church and in the general body of believers today who do not actively support a vision that embraces a model of church compatible with Vatican II's vision. This is primarily the root of the cause for so much destructive tension in the church today.

But, I dream of a church that will have leaders from pope to laity and everyone in between creating a spirit of real collegiality among the faithful. I dream of a church where all of us will be free and empowered to come together and discern what the Holy Spirit is inspiring us to create. I dream of a church that will create a vision for the future by being more responsive to Jesus' call to "Come, follow me" instead of being led by restrictive and legalistic ideologies. I dream of a church in *transformation*, not *change*.

CHAPTER 9

A New Creation, But Not "Window Dressing"

• • • • • •

The theologian will observe that human relations have a religious significance and are under God's eye. But people will not refuse to adopt their lived experience as a touchstone and, on pain of degrading religion to a daydream, they are ultimately obliged to admit that principles and inner life are alibis the moment they cease to animate external and everyday life.

Maurice Merleau-Ponty

• • • • • •

Change in structures of an organization often can be used as merely an exercise in window dressing in an organization's appearance rather than to create a newly transformed institution whose culture and character is renewed at its core. It is clear that to become the pilgrim church that we still are, we Catholics must become a new creation—in love with our Creator, our church, our leaders, our fellow members, and the entire world. In other words, we should take seriously Merleau-Ponty's admonition above that all of us, from the pope to the layperson hanging on to the church by his or her fingernails, are "... obliged to admit that principles and inner life are alibis the moment our lived experience ceases to animate external and everyday life."

However, there seems to be a proclivity among many of the members of the institutional church's hierarchy to approach how they operate and relate to the faithful with a distorted and dualistic western bias that does not convincingly integrate divine/spiritual and human/secular realities. This organizational culture contributes to existing tensions in the church and constrains its relevance in today's globalized world. Too often, we the faithful see many of our leaders more concerned with promulgating rules and regulations for others to follow than with helping the lives of the people they are serving. When fair-minded people judge the institutional church's actions as wrong or inappropriate in a secular/human sense, the institutional church leaders too easily resort to insisting on their teaching's divine/spiritual dimension. This worked for a long time, until the systematic cover-up of pedophilia by many in the institutional church (fairly and appropriately documented in the popular movie *Spotlight*) blew the lid off that particular attitude.

For instance, in the case of the almost universal moral acceptance by faithful childbearing-age Catholics for some forms of artificial birth control, the official doctrine still insists it is always and objectively sinful. The hierarchy's response is that they are correct in teaching only natural family planning because they are divinely inspired with the truth. They give little credence to the lived experience of the People of God, who are *also* inspired by the Holy Spirit. Unlike unmarried clerics, it is lay couples who actually live a life of intimacy with a married partner and have to grapple with the loving question of how many children they should have and when to have them. In other words, married couples live Natural Law; and the rest of us need to listen to their experience. The Holy Spirit does not inspire just the clerical hierarchy in the church with grace-filled wisdom about human sexuality. That would be absurd to believe.

The hierarchy stresses the special gifts that they (i.e. the pope and the bishops) are given by God. In this regard, they love to quote this passage from Vatican II that emphasizes that divine/spiritual dimension:

Therefore, the Sacred Council teaches that bishops by divine institution have succeeded to the place of the apostles as shepherds of the church, and he who hears them, hears Christ, and he who rejects them, rejects Christ and Him who sent Christ.

Lumen Gentium, 20

Of course, some of my female friends claim that because the Council used the male pronoun exclusively in the above passage, none of it applies to them, but I assure them that this is just a matter of poor translation! That is why throughout this book I have "corrected" the translation of Vatican documents to include women as well as men.

Now, we all know that we can quote from most church documents and emphasize whatever point that we are trying to make. Nevertheless, sometimes it is important to stress some passages that help bring to light a fuller context of doctrine not usually emphasized by some in church leadership. Clearly, I have been selective in my quoting of church documents, but it is with the intention of presenting a more nuanced and subtler understanding of church teaching regarding the question of whether we are after a new creation of the church or just providing some new window dressing for a tired institution.

There are many members of the church leadership who give the impression that they are pontificating (literally "acting like the pope") when they proclaim, in effect: The church is unity, but it is not a democracy; we decree, you obey; that's our definition of unity. But they do not reflect what was made clear by Vatican II: The church is made one not because of any inherent power or authority they have. The church is unified when it is "...a people made one with the unity of the Father, the Son, and the Holy Spirit" (*Lumen Gentium,* 1.4).

Isn't it about time that all of us finally wake up to the essence of Christianity—the love Jesus modeled for all to see? Christian *oneness* is not secular *sameness.* Christian oneness is modeled on the divine diversity that is the Holy Trinity. Apparently, God rejected sameness and decided divine oneness is found only in the diversity of three different and distinct divine Persons. If that kind of unity is good enough for God, why isn't it good enough for the church? Our leaders should be shepherds that accept, support, and joyfully encourage the diversity of the People of God, rather than trying to impose a sameness they control.

The curious point in all of this, though, is that we Catholics still have faith that the church truly is divinely established and inspired. We have faith that the ordained are called to serve and are divinely gifted with grace to do so. We also have faith, however, that we lay people and vowed religious are also divinely gifted as followers of Christ to discern the Spirit of God. No one in the church has a monopoly on wisdom…or sanctity.

But how can we be a church that is organized and structured to be both a spiritual and a worldly institutional reality? How can we be a church committed to transformation and ushering in a new creation? Is that even possible? My short answer is "yes." My long answer is "yes, but with great difficulty." (You should not be surprised at this answer).

If we approach a solution to these important questions by equating the *church* with the *institutional church* (i.e., its structures and hierarchy) then this is a non-starter. All of us in the church must fully accept that a solution to the problems of the church does not lie in putting in place new structures, offices, and committees in the human organizational entity. Transformation must happen first in the vision, imagination, and culture of how we can be *one* in the Catholic Church of the twenty-first century. The divine mystery of the church is that Jesus established the reality of his kingdom here on earth: "The church, or, in other words, the kingdom of Christ now present in mystery, grows visibly through the power of God in the world" (*Lumen Gentium,* 1.3).

However, Jesus was not incarnated into this world with a specific human organizational structure that accompanied him from heaven. The point I underscore here is not in any way to question that from the beginning Jesus did empower his disciples with the responsibility and grace to serve a divinely inspired church. But Jesus did not leave them with a set structure that needed no further development. Rather, he left them with the Holy Spirit.

Note

No reasonable interpretation of Scripture or Tradition would claim that Jesus (or the early disciples) established an organizational structure that even remotely resembles today's institutional church: its hierarchy, its rules and regulations, or its *modus operandi*. How the church is organized today is the result of human dynamics embedded in the different ways and forms that play a role in any societal organizational development. Yes, Peter was succeeded by popes and the apostles by bishops. But the church is also a communion of all believers, the People of God, inspired by the Holy Spirit, and served—not ruled—by leaders who are successors of Peter and the early disciples. The different roles in ministry within the one body of the church are for service to all. No one— no pope, no cardinal, no bishop, no monsignor, no priest, no curia official— controls the workings and inspiration of the Holy Spirit in the hearts and minds of the faithful. This is the divine mystery of the one, holy, catholic, and apostolic church, and no other explanation is necessary.

The institutional church is not, in and of itself, the Catholic Church. It is a human/worldly evolving organization, with leaders who "…endowed with sacred power, serve the faithful so that all who are of the People of God, and therefore enjoy a true Christian dignity, working toward a common goal freely and in an orderly way, may arrive at salvation (*Lumen Gentium*, 3.18).

Clearly it is not the Vatican (i.e., its organization, structures, and ways of conducting matters in service to the entire church, including all the faithful) that has a fullness and comprehensive sacred or divine status:

> *The head of the church is Christ. He is the image of the invisible God and in him all things came into being. He is before all creatures and in him all things hold together. He is the head of the Body that is the church.*

> *Lumen Gentium*, 1.7

church as a new creation is certainly not something that has become
just in the twenty-first century. Throughout its two-thousand-year history, the institutional church evolved in its organization to meet the different
needs and circumstances of the people and of the times. Today we are in a
globalized society in which technology and transportation has brought diverse
peoples, cultures, and religions together. The world, as we say, is "shrinking!"

• • • • • •

These prerequisites for being a "good" Catholic simply do not match the spirit of love and mercy introduced into this world by Jesus—no matter how hard you try to spin it.

• • • • • •

The Catholic Church is also becoming globalized and shrinking before our eyes. Just as this
reality has not brought peace and harmony
among the nations of the world; neither has it
brought religions closer together in understanding and acceptance; nor has it been a cause that
has facilitated communion, even among Catholics worldwide or within dioceses.

The church simply cannot stay with a mind-
set, culture, practices, and behavior that worked
in the past. True, there are some Catholic traditionalists within the hierarchy and laity who are
staunch and nostalgic supporters of a past era
with regal pageantry in liturgy; with docile ac-
quiescence to the hierarchy; with a preference for defined rules and regulations;
with making certain that women are never to be ordained into the ministerial
priesthood; with a determination that no non-traditional life-styles between
loving persons are permitted to the sacraments; and with a significant bias to
western culture for all in the church, even if it is not relevant to non-western
Catholics. But these prerequisites for being a "good" Catholic no longer reso-
nate with most people today—especially young people, who are the future of
our church. Such prerequisites simply do not match the spirit of love and mercy
introduced into this world by Jesus—no matter how hard you try to spin it.

Understanding what *is* today, and what *was* yesterday, dictates that there is
a great need for the Holy Spirit to inspire the People of God to what *will be* tomorrow. The alienation of many Catholics is not difficult to perceive. Even the
institutional church acknowledges this, as evidenced by their increasing em-

phasis on what Saint Pope John Paul II called the "New Evangelization," aimed at calling former practicing Catholics back to the pews. However, what is not perceived by many is that the root cause of the problem of church attendance is the failure of the institutional church leaders to effectively transform their own culture and embrace the broad range of new experiences, new knowledge, and growing diversity of expressions of faith among the People of God throughout the world.

Rigid traditionalists in the church—clergy, hierarchy, vowed religious, and laity alike—claim that the church does not need to be newly created. This reluctance to transform the church seems to indicate a profound misunderstanding of the role of societal and cultural forces that are entwined in the inspired imaginations of the People of God. This comes from their lack of appreciation for the fact that Jesus gave the Holy Spirit not just to clerics but to all his followers who live a faith-filled life in the many different cultures throughout the world.

This important worldly understanding of societal forces unfolds a better appreciation of the dynamics of how we grasp and reach the spiritual forces unleashed by Jesus. Again, it is not because of some magic that the People of God have Christian faith. Rather, God chose to become flesh to introduce us to the vision of unconditional love for all. That vision is the mission of the church, and anything that gets in the way of that vision must be changed or done away with. I believe this human phenomenon and an insight into its importance was effectively captured by one of the most distinguished philosophers of the twentieth century, Paul Ricoeur (1913-2005) in his book, *History and Truth*:

> *Yet the profound meaning of the institution appears only when it is extended to the images of humans in culture, literature, and the arts. The images have indeed been constituted or established. They have stability and an internal history that transcend the chance happenings of the individual. Their structure may be subjected to psychoanalysis of the imagination, which would analyze the persuasive theme of these images of people, their lives of force, and their evolution. It is in this sense that culture is established at the level of the tradition of the imaginary.*

If the image of the Catholic Church remains under the control of those with a worldview in which rigid, fragmented and categorical approaches to the essence of what it means to be church remains entrenched, then the church cannot make Jesus real or meaningful for today's people. That would be a sin.

But I dream of a church in which all levels of authority and all the faithful are so divinely inspired that they never hesitate or fear to place Jesus' love for the person above any rule, law, or dictum. I dream of a church that is a new creation that imagines, models, and animates the twenty-first century world with the spirit of Jesus' acceptance, inclusion, and unconditional love for all. I dream that the new creation of Jesus' spirit for today's church comes in my lifetime and that I can help bring it to fruition. I dream of loving mercy from God, not justification from the canons of rules and laws.

CHAPTER 10

We Need New Structures, But It Won't Be Easy

· · · · · ·

Life cannot wait until the sciences may have explained the universe scientifically. We cannot put off living until we are ready. The most salient characteristic of life is its coerciveness; it is always urgent, "here and now," without any possible postponement.

JOSE ORTEGA Y GASSET

· · · · · ·

There is a unique (perhaps "sarcastic" is a more accurate descriptor) attitude many Catholics around the world have that portrays our institutional church leaders as never being wrong...just taking a very, very long time to get it right! However, today's globalized world has, in the words of Thomas Friedman, somehow become "flatter": Distance has been shortened; time moves faster; and communication is now instantaneous. Patience, passiveness, and perseverance just do not seem to be as virtuous as they were in days gone by. Indeed, Ortega y Gasset's observation above has never been more apropos: "The most salient characteristic of life is its coerciveness; it is always urgent, 'here and now,' without any possible postponement."

In fact for many of us, the more than fifty-year postponement of serious transformation in the Catholic Church since Saint Pope John XXIII "opened the windows" at Vatican Council II is an embarrassment to the venerated memory of this great saint. Only now, five decades later, is Pope Francis trying to re-open those very same windows. We are beginning to see some fresh air again blowing into the Vatican halls and stirring the red birettas on the heads of some in the curia. Unfortunately, every once in a while we again spot some of them attempting to close those windows, or at least lowering them so that not too much fresh air will sweep in.

With all the recent unrest evident inside the institutional church, it certainly is not disloyal or disrespectful to acknowledge that the church is experiencing some unhealthy turmoil. It is obvious to conservatives, moderates, and progressives alike that there is a growing dissonance about how some church leaders operate; how the rest of us think they should operate; and what structural changes should be made in the church to respond to the needs of the twenty-first century.

But is there a "one and only" new structure for the institutional church that will solve the present day turmoil? And am I, an ordinary De La Salle Christian Brother, the one to propose it?

My short answer is "no." My longer answer is "definitely not!"

Fortunately, we see that Pope Francis has set in motion the dynamics for institutional and operational changes in the offices at the Vatican. He has set up committees to study and recommend structural changes that will help the Vatican's institutional infrastructure be more responsive to modern day church needs; to be more responsible, accountable, and transparent to the People of God and to the world; and to operate more efficiently and pastorally. Already some new organizational restructuring has taken place.

However, what all must understand when assessing if particular changes will be effective in transforming the institutional church into the church that I have been am describing is another story. It's another story because the structural/organizational specifics alone will not cause the transformation we crave and demand; rather, transformation will only occur when we the church—hierarchy, bureaucracy, clergy, and laity alike—finally pull together to transform our church culture and imagine a new creation of the church that is much closer to the church that Jesus founded upon his "rock."

Paul Ricoeur said so poignantly: "Every real conversion is first a revolution at the level of our directive images. By changing their imagination, humans alter their existence." I am not so naïve that I do not recognize that the governance of the Catholic Church is intimately interwoven with canonical issues and entrenched structures that have been firmly established over time. Of course attempts to change traditional and ingrained practices are difficult; but these undertakings are even more resistive to renewal when the leaders of the existing governance structures try to adopt the patina of holy inevitability. I am not so simple-minded and gullible to not understand that these canonical and organizational structures and systems are transformable only if there develops in the hearts and minds of the hierarchy a *metanoia*, i.e., a "conversion," to a truly collegial vision of the church that does not fear to place Jesus' love for the person above any laws and institutional structures.

Unless and until our institutional church leaders, fueled by the faithful's perceptions and expectations, see a radical new vision for the church as Jesus lived and taught, all that we will accomplish is to fool ourselves into believing that our church has been transformed. Jesus taught his followers that it was not the laws that reveal his Father in heaven, but it is our witness to God's love that God's kingdom comes "on earth, as it is in heaven."

A complementary insight into this truth was powerfully stated in 1975 by Pope Paul VI:

Modern people listen more willingly to witnesses than to teachers, and if they do listen to teachers, it is because those teachers are witnesses. It is therefore primarily by her conduct and by her life that the church will evangelize the world, in other words, by her living witness of fidelity to the Lord Jesus—the witness of poverty and detachment, of freedom in the face of the powers of this world, in short, the witness of sanctity.

Apostolic Exhortation, *Evangelii Nuntiandi*
(*Evangelization in the Modern World*), 41

There is obviously no "one and only" structure that will be or could be the solution for our church's needed transformation. Of course, Pope Francis' initiation of organizational changes in the Vatican's curia is quite helpful, but alone those changes will not be the solution. I have already acknowledged the incomparable uniqueness of the Catholic Church in its human realization as an institutional structure and its concurrent spiritual realization as a divinely instituted holy People of God. So no one is advocating throwing the proverbial baby out with the proverbial bathwater. But, let's face it, folks, we need new structures for our church, and we need them fast, and it's not going to be easy to get them.

Pope Paul VI had the right answer, in my humble (? !) opinion: The one, holy, catholic, and apostolic church exists as a spiritual reality to the extent that it is "…by her living witness of fidelity to the Lord Jesus—the witness of poverty and detachment, of freedom in the face of the powers of this world, in short, the witness of sanctity." No one, not even the most entrenched bureaucrat or self-righteous bishop, would disagree that we need a new church structure incorporating the use of best practices and processes to help the entire People of God carry out our mission fairly, justly, transparently, and with accountability.

• • • • • •

We need a new church structure incorporating the use of best practices and processes to help the entire People of God carry out our mission fairly, justly, transparently, and with accountability.

• • • • • •

The hierarchy cannot operate as if the special blessings of ordination or episcopacy exempt them from good, sound human dynamics and interactions. New structures—whatever they will be—will only be helpful to the degree that the hearts and minds of those who lead us transform their very notion of themselves from controllers of an institution into leaders (or shepherds, if you must) of the entire People of God.

Father Thomas Reese in his March 6, 2015, article in the *National Catholic Reporter* captured this observation powerfully when he wrote:

> *Many observers do not recognize how revolutionary is the change in style and culture that Pope Francis is calling for. It is more important than moving around boxes on the organizational chart. The difficulty is that it requires buy-in by bishops and clergy throughout the world. There will be no "Francis effect" unless hearts and attitudes are changed. Too many seminarians and young priests see themselves as correctors of lay laxity and heterodoxy rather than as companions in a pilgrimage to the Lord....*
>
> *The church is not the pope. Unless bishops, priests, and laity follow his example and embrace his priorities, there will not be permanent change in the church. The temptations to clericalism and self-centeredness are too strong. We have to stop admiring the pope and start imitating him.*

It is my contention that since there is not one and only one perfect new structure that will transform the church, we should all take Father Reese's advice and start imitating Pope Francis—his spirit, his mercy, his sensitivity, his compassion, and his desire for openness and freedom and dialogue in the church.

There are many different and effective models that could be put into place that would transform the entire organizational culture and dynamics of the church. A book (many books!) could be written to suggest various models. This is not one of those books. I will share some attributes in the next chapter that I believe could help us judge whether changes are just window dressing or are transformative. But before we get into specifics about what the structures of a new Catholic Church might look like, there is still that *metanoia* (change of heart) thing to be accomplished.

Most current organizational dynamics books or management consultants insist that all organizations in the burgeoning new global world society must initiate a paradigm shift in their institutional culture regarding how they operate and how they understand their very existence and mission. Such a paradigm shift (a radical change in underlying beliefs or theory) has been touted *ad nauseum* in the lexicon of management theory in recent decades. Though that trendy nomenclature finally became annoying, the underlying need for organizations to transform how they perceive themselves has embedded itself in the very fiber of modern effective institutions. Why would the Catholic Church not require a paradigm change? A change in the mind-set of leaders in any institution, but especially in the Catholic Church, whose culture and *modus operandi* have been cemented into its very institutional core, is essential if there is to be any hope at transformation.

Now, here is the secret formula for successful institutional change: Common sense must inform institutional forms. In other words, when changes in the culture in which an institution operates have qualitatively transformed how people act, react, and interact, institutions must change their structures or else they relegate themselves to the ash heap of history. It is necessary for an institution to make itself structurally effective and efficient if it is to be successful in fulfilling its mission. In today's globalized world, all institutions, including religious ones, are compelled to change the way they deliver their message in the face of the evolution of values, technologies, communications, and aspirations of a transformed world.

The problem in the institutional church today seems to be that some are mistaking its traditional hierarchical form of governance with the essence of the core message and mission of the church. They seem to act almost as if they equate changing the traditional structures of the institutional church with changing the core Gospel message and mission of the church, which is to spread the Good News of God's unconditional love for us and our unconditional love for our neighbors.

Changing the structures of the institutional church today is not a suggestion, it is an imperative. This is not because transformation of institutions is the latest fad in the organizational dynamics marketplace; rather it is because the church must speak to and witness to people who live today and not to those who might have lived in some glorified past that never actually existed.

If an imperious hierarchical structure ("princes of the church," really?) is embedded in our Catholic imagination, then controlling power instead of serving authority will be our paradigm. We Catholics need a paradigm that celebrates and supports our magnificent diversity, cultures, life styles, and common sense. And we deserve structures that serve that paradigm.

I believe a "strange loop" exists in the governance structure of today's institutional church and is a significant cause of many of our criticisms falling on deaf ears in the Vatican and dioceses throughout the world. I borrow this "strange loop" image from Douglas R. Hofstadter's popular book, first published back in 1980, *Gödel, Escher, Bach: An Eternal Golden Braid*. In this intriguing book Hofstadter utilizes his study of K. Gödel's mathematics, M.C. Escher's art, and J.S. Bach's music to understand the effects of a hierarchical mind-set and culture on people and institutions. Hofstadter explained:

> *The "Strange Loop" phenomenon occurs whenever by moving upwards (or downwards) through the levels of some hierarchical system, we unexpectedly find ourselves right back where we started…. Sometimes I use the term Tangled Hierarchy to describe a system in which strange loops occur. As we go on, the theme of Strange Loops will recur again and again. Sometimes it will be hidden, other times it will be out in the open; sometimes it will be right side up, other times it will be upside down, or backwards. "Quaerendo invenietis" is my advice to the reader.*

It is helpful to take Hofstadter's advice as we talk about changing the structures of the Catholic Church: *Quaerendo invenietis*, i.e. "By seeking you will discover." It seems to me that as there are attempts to develop new structures for the institutional church, it is essential that we first investigate the dynamics within the strange loops of the institutional church's hierarchical systems and claims to power. If we are to truly transform how we will be a church in the twenty-first century and serve a twenty-first-century people who no longer live in medieval times (or even in the twentieth century), then we must break away from the current "Tangled Hierarchy" and transform the very structure of today's institutional church.

Of course this transformation of the church will not happen in a few weeks, a few months, or a few years. However, it cannot take decades! Let us not deceive ourselves that because the Church has been around for two thousand years it can take all the time it wants before being responsive to the *sensus fidei*. Hear again Ortega y Gasset's insight that began this chapter: "The most salient characteristic of life is its coerciveness; it is always urgent, 'here and now,' without any possible postponement."

In this globalized world, time has taken on a qualitatively new dimension of urgency. Many current leaders of the institutional church do not agree and are only willing to accept small, incremental, "window-dressing" changes. Thank God that Pope Francis is not one of them.

I dream of a church that continuously seeks to discover new structures through the inspiration and promptings of the Holy Spirit so that it may be better responsive to the needs of the People of God in the "here and now." I dream of church leaders who embrace their vocations to serve by enabling the People of God to respond freely to Jesus' Gospel rather than church leaders who are part of a strange loop of hierarchical prerogatives that justifies their privilege, control, and power. And I dream of a church that moves boldly into the twenty-first century by reading the signs of the times and transforming how it operates.

CHAPTER 11

The Simple, But Not-So-Secret, Recipe for a Transformed Church

• • • • • •

*Jesus does not give recipes that show the way to God
as other teachers of religion do. He is himself the way.*

KARL BARTH

• • • • • •

If we agree that there is not one ideal structure that will satisfy all the difficulties encountered by our Catholic Church today, are we foolish to even attempt to transform how it operates? The complex dynamics found in even a simple secular institution do not lend themselves to a singular organizational model.

I think I have proven convincingly in this book (at least I have convinced myself) that when Jesus established his church he did not lay down an organizational chart with a schematic design for a clerical/curial structure. In fact, most theologians assert that such a model would have been the last model Jesus would have initiated. As Karl Barth observes above, Jesus "is himself the way."

Yet many faithful church observers understand that to transform the institutional church there must be an open, transparent, and candid exploration of the "strange loops" of hierarchical practices and claims of power that have attached themselves like barnacles to the church's governance structures over the centuries. This phenomenon has crescendoed today as more and more of us cry out, "Why doesn't the institutional church practice what it preaches?"

The quick answer is that the church as an institution never has, never will, and is incapable of practicing what it preaches. Only real live human beings who are followers of Jesus of Nazareth and faithful members of his church can do that.

A more pointed and jarring assessment than mine about the problems in the institutional church was given by Cardinal Carlo Maria Martini, a Jesuit and the Archbishop of Milan from 1979 to 2002. He said in his last public interview on August 8, 2012, two weeks before he died:

> *Our culture has become old, our churches and our religious houses are big and empty, the bureaucratic apparatus of the church grows, our rites and our dress are pompous.... The church is 200 years behind the times.*

Is there a recipe that will give us the ingredients for a new structure for the institutional church that will effectively solve these ensnaring and destructive problems? The answer is, as you might expect from me by now, "yes...but...."

The simple recipe that I suggest here presents the most important ingredients that should be the hallmarks of the church of the twenty-first century. One might say I give a recipe that includes all the ingredients for a cake, but I don't tell you the exact proportions, how to mix them together, or for how long to bake it.

I believe this is a more realistic approach, since the many specific alternatives for feasible organizational structures for the Catholic Church could invite the publication of a countless number of other books. At this point, because of the refreshing spirit infused by Pope Francis, the church may better benefit from a recipe of "qualities to be included" upon which to judge the efficacy of any specific structural models that have already been or will be initiated. I strongly urge us to not accept "window-dressing" changes that do nothing to transform the core culture of clericalism in the institutional church.

In fact, I present a recipe with only three ingredients that should be thoroughly folded and mixed into any and every proposed structural change that would create a new model or even specific operational changes for the church. Of course there are many more ingredients that should go into this recipe, but I choose these three since I am convinced that these three basic concepts, if correctly understood and applied, will ensure that the many other ingredients that may be added at a later time will enhance the end result.

I also ask you to heed another of Karl Barth's insights as you assess my three proposed basic ingredients, when he said, "Faith in God's revelation has nothing to do with an ideology that glorifies the status quo." Not to heed Barth's insight is to literally condemn the People of God to an ineffective and petrified institutional church, a cult stuck in a nostalgic past of clericalism, paternalism, and misogyny.

The First Ingredient for a New Church Structure

A REALISTIC ENVIRONMENTAL SCAN

As the new globalized world matures, it is bringing cultural, societal, economic, and religious diversity to the forefront by causing more, not fewer, clashes of misunderstanding and intolerance. This resulting discord, combined with recent and ongoing media-hyped scandals, contributes to a significant diminishment of the institutional church's influence as a beacon of light in a world in dire need of Jesus' message.

All of this makes it essential that we all make decisions about our church structures based on what are called "environmental scanned world facts" and not on pious and often repeated exhortations made in incomprehensible (at least to the non-religious professionals among us) language. A more spiritual label for a relevant, realistic, and responsive environmental scan is "reading the signs of the times," the wonderful phrase from Vatican II that traces its origin all the way back to Jesus. It comes from the Gospel of Matthew. Here is the translation from *The Message* by Eugene Peterson:

Some Pharisees and Sadducees were on him again, pressing him to prove himself to them. He told them, "You have a saying that goes, 'Red sky at night, sailor's delight; red sky at morning, sailors take warning.' You find it easy enough to forecast the weather—why can't you read the signs of the times?"

Matthew 16:1-3, *The Message*

The point of doing a realistic environmental scan for religious leaders is that it does not allow for biased attitudes, preconceived conclusions, or pious judgments. As Karl Barth also warned, "Faith is never identical with piety."

It seems to me that an objective global environmental scan demonstrates that the Catholic Church, relatively speaking, is out of step on a variety of issues from gender equality to sexuality to new forms of family relationships. On the other hand, the Catholic Church is a leader in issues regarding the sanctity of life; religious liberty; and social justice for immigrants, the disabled, and the poor. On the issue of religious practice, we are admired for our strong contemplative tradition, the beauty of our liturgies and music, and our commitment to education. We are not so admired for our emphasis on orthodoxy, our denial of communion to those who do not agree with us, and certainly our cover-ups of our own institutional failures.

We could go on and on, but the point is this: Can we build on our strengths and minimize our weaknesses as we try to spread the Good News of Jesus Christ? Or must we fight doctrinal issues in every fight as if it is a matter of life and death? Can we be "all things to all people" or must all people buy the whole enchilada before we can even begin a dialogue with them?

This then is the first ingredient in a recipe that we Catholics must use as we attempt to transform our church structures: We must honestly look at an environmental scan pointing to the signs of the times and seek to do an objective analysis of where we stand and how we need to proceed. It will do us no good to bring our pious or biased ideological baggage on our journey to transform our church.

The Second Ingredient for a New Church Structure

BE MORE CATHOLIC, BUT WITH A SMALL "C"

I am convinced that once the first ingredient of a healthy portion of environmental scan is added to our recipe for structural change in our church, the next ingredient is to add a big dollop of being catholic with a small "c" that will help remedy the current deteriorating standing of our institutional church leaders.

Blaming others who don't agree with us, whether inside or outside the church, for our problems in the church today is not a solution to those problems. It's an excuse for not tackling them. Be honest: Jesus never required a fixed degree of piety, a specific philosophy, or an orthodox theology in order to be his follower. He never limited who was worthy to follow him to those who could explain the Holy Trinity or the Real Presence or the Assumption of Mary. The church that Jesus established is for everyone, at every time, in every culture. It is *catholic* in that sense and must not be limited by anyone trying to control it or impose some culturally conditioned theology or philosophy. Let me say it as clearly as I can: Enough with using only Western culture's myths, metaphors, and models as if they are theological and philosophical truths established by Jesus or inspired by the Holy Spirit.

What makes us universal is when people who think differently from us ask "Where do you live?" that we answer, as Jesus did, "Come and see," and then proceed to enter into a mutually respectful dialogue with them. If they are forced to be irreversibly orthodox in their views before they can do so, or if we are not open to their ideas, thoughts, and life styles, then it is (sorry) only window-dressing openness.

Changes in church structures must consider that evangelization in a globally diverse world cannot be an attempt to bring people to a culturally rigid organizational entity within the symbolic walls of the Vatican; but rather, evangelization is to bring Jesus to people by folding the world's diversity into communion with the People of God. We must never forget: True evangelization is not bringing people to the institutional church. It is bringing Jesus to the people. This is the true totality of the "catholic" church. Reflecting again on Cardinal Martini's final interview, we should take to heart what he said:

> *I advise the pope and the bishops to seek out twelve people outside the lines for administrative positions, people who are close to the poorest, who are surrounded by young people, and who try new things. We need to be with people who burn in such a way that the Spirit can spread itself everywhere.*

That is what being catholic was for Jesus; must be for the global reality of today's People of God; and must be for the future of the church.

The Third Ingredient for a New Church Structure

WOMEN

Yes, simply women. More of them. In positions of power. Taken seriously. Ordained. Named bishops and cardinals. Elected pope. This third ingredient finishes this basic foundational recipe for changing the structure of our church, and it is the most important of the three.

Now, before I am run out of Rome on a rail, at least hear me out. The first argument, of course, is simple equality. As Paul said in the letter to the Galatians:

> *In Christ's family there can be no division into Jew and non-Jew, slave and free, male and female. Among us you are all equal. That is, we are all in a common relationship with Jesus Christ. Also, since you are Christ's*

*family, then you are Abraham's famous "descendant," heirs according to
the covenant promises.*

Galatians 3:28-29, The Message

So if our recipe for a new church structure is based on reading the signs of
the times and trying to be as "small-c" catholic as we can, then women simply
must be a part of it in a real and powerful way. If they are not, then any new
structure will fail.

What about other groups that are not part of the existing institutional
church structure, you might ask? Yes, there are other issues with representa-
tion in the church leadership, and those too need
to be dealt with. But women are the only group
that some church leaders are actively trying to
exclude from church leadership, claiming that it
is all Jesus' fault! This of course is ridiculous and
is ridiculed, but the fact is that so far they are
succeeding in barring women from ordination,
so this issue cannot be ignored in any discussion
of a new church structure.

> • • • • • •
>
> *Women are the only
> group that some church
> leaders are actively
> trying to exclude from
> church leadership,
> claiming that it is all
> Jesus' fault!*
>
> • • • • • •

For beyond the question of equality and fair-
ness, there is a much more important reason that
women have to be one of the three basic ingredients of any new church structure. That reason
is that women are different from men (in case
you haven't noticed). Women have different ways from men of imagining and
describing and reacting and responding to things, and the church needs their
insight and leadership as it moves forward into the twenty-first century.

Many people have pointed out that had women had real positions in church
leadership, the pedophilia crisis in the church would never have reached the
proportions it did. I am one of them.

In my first draft of writing about this basic ingredient in new church structure, I started with this sentence: "I am a man so I really cannot credibly speak
for or about women's role in the church." But, when I finished the first draft and

reviewed it, I realized that, if we are going to get gender role issues corrected in the church, both women *and* men better speak up; otherwise we too will be guilty of a culturally conditioned prejudice (one partly caused by the Catholic Church itself) that is destructive to the entire People of God and to the entire world.

Furthermore, the current male-dominated clericalist culture is significantly detrimental to men also, since it is an abuse of power within the very infrastructure of the church. Insisting that women and men in the church must have different roles because they have male or female body parts is to perpetuate a defective and biased theology, flouting Christian common sense and divine revelation. It's about time this silliness stops!

Any theology, institutional or canonical legalisms, or erudite explanations that say otherwise should not be acceptable to the People of God. If the leaders of the institutional church continue to insist that we the faithful cannot even discuss the question of women's ordination, then the church is doomed to a patriarchal prejudice that equates Christian authority and truth with clericalism in its most devastating and destructive incarnation. It has got to stop, and it has got to stop now.

But I dream of a church that is organized and structured in a way that welcomes all—not just the many and certainly not just the few—and witnesses to all the unconditional love that *"becomes all things to all people."* I dream of a church where all are included in all roles and all sacraments are open to all. I call this the "one, holy, catholic, and apostolic" church.

CHAPTER 12

No Closure, But What...?

· · · · · ·

The theological virtue of hope is the patient and trustful willingness to live without closure, without resolution, and still be content and even happy because our Satisfaction is now at another level, and our Source is beyond ourselves.

RICHARD ROHR, OFM

· · · · · ·

Whenever important challenges come into our lives, we seek a successful conclusion in which all problems are solved nice and tidily. It seems to me that such a favorable ending is expected even more so when religion is involved. After all, the faithful adherents of a particular religion believe they have God on their side.

But for the Catholic People of God, getting closure on the demand to lovingly serve is never completely possible. Historically, any ostensible answer to the difficult challenges within the evolving institutional church has always proven to be illusory, because Christian love infuses the desire for holy perfection into a world of human imperfection that always begets new problems and further challenges.

I point out that this was as true in Jesus' time as it is in our own. Yet he ends the Sermon on the Mount by telling us: "Be perfect, therefore, as your heavenly Father is perfect" (Matthew 5:48, *NRSV*). I have always thought this to be one of the stranger precepts of Jesus. How in this world are we to be perfect, and not just perfect but as perfect as the Father? Eugene Peterson's *The Message* has helped me understand what Jesus means. Here is how the Sermon on the Mount ends in that contemporary translation:

"And don't say anything you don't mean. This counsel is embedded deep in our traditions. You only make things worse when you lay down a smoke screen of pious talk, saying, 'I'll pray for you,' and never doing it, or saying, 'God be with you,' and not meaning it. You don't make your words true by embellishing them with religious lace. In making your speech sound more religious, it becomes less true. Just say 'yes' and 'no.' When you manipulate words to get your own way, you go wrong.

"Here's another old saying that deserves a second look: 'Eye for eye, tooth for tooth.' Is that going to get us anywhere? Here's what I propose: 'Don't hit back at all.' If someone strikes you, stand there and take it. If someone drags you into court and sues for the shirt off your back, gift-wrap your best coat and make a present of it. And if someone takes unfair advantage of you, use the occasion to practice the servant life. No more tit-for-tat stuff. Live generously.

"You're familiar with the old written law, 'Love your friend,' and its unwritten companion, 'Hate your enemy.' I'm challenging that. I'm telling you to love your enemies. Let them bring out the best in you, not the worst. When someone gives you a hard time, respond with the energies of prayer, for then you are working out of your true selves, your God-created selves. This is what God does. He gives his best—the sun to warm and the rain to nourish—to everyone, regardless: the good and bad, the nice and nasty. If all you do is love the lovable, do you expect a bonus? Anybody can do that. If you simply say hello to those who greet you, do you expect a medal? Any run-of-the-mill sinner does that.

"In a word, what I'm saying is, Grow up. You're kingdom subjects. Now live like it. Live out your God-created identity. Live generously and graciously toward others, the way God lives toward you."

Matthew 5:33-48, *The Message*

This is how the People of God must embrace the change we need. We must become all things to all people, and in order to do that we have to "grow up." We are "kingdom subjects" and we need to start acting like it. In that way, and only in that way, will we be perfect as our heavenly Father is perfect.

Now, it would be naïve to believe that all the challenges to solving the church's current turmoil will be overcome in our lifetime. True, Pope Francis—fifty years since Vatican II—has once again opened the windows in the institutional church. Yet even he has indicated that his papacy will be short, and none of us know who will replace him. So a realistic discernment of the wonderful phenomenon of Francis compels us to heed Father Rohr's insight above: to have Christian hope is the "patient and trustful willingness to live without closure, without resolution, and still be content and even happy because our Satisfaction is now at another level, and our Source is beyond ourselves."

I am firmly convinced that with this kind of Christian hope we as the People of God will be able to endure and confront the difficulties I have elaborated in this book and help effect the transformation essential to transform our beloved church into one that Jesus intended us to be. To do so, we need to "just say *yes* and *no*," and stop trying to manipulate one another. We need to love our enemies, both inside and outside the church, and let them bring out the best in us, not the worst. We need to not hit back at all, but to stand there and take it. "No more tit-for-tat stuff" for us. We need to live generously.

Even though there will surely be other challenges that still remain in our church and others that will arise, we need to remain in "communion" with the church. While I certainly understand the dissatisfaction experienced by many with certain actions of and scandals within the institutional church, I believe that to leave the company of the People of God out of frustration with some of our leaders is not the correct option, at least for most of us. We must remember that the Catholic Church is not the pope's, the Vatican's, or the hierarchy's church. It is all of ours. We are rock, and the even the gates of hell cannot prevail against us!

Believe me, I certainly have many as-yet-unfulfilled dreams for the church, but I do not live in some pious fantasy world (if you have read this book so far, I guess "pious" is not a descriptor you would use for my convictions) as if I were blinded by hallucinations and fantasies that arise from exorbitant euphoria. I believe I have hope-filled dreams that will help Jesus' love live long in his church.

I am just as upset as many are, for example, when an actual cardinal of the Catholic Church publically states that he is convinced that a significant cause for a shortage of priests today is that boys are "turned-off" because girls are allowed to be altar servers. I want to scream; then I want to laugh; and then I want to cry. Not because His Eminence is so mistaken, which he is, but because I fear he is sincere! What I am most concerned about is why his fellow cardinals have not challenged him on such an absurd statement. Their silence is more outrageous than his statement.

Another archbishop attempts to control Catholic school teachers' adherence to his elaboration of orthodoxy with an emphasis on sexual issues by changing their contractual obligations in the faculty handbook. He insists that teachers may not take public positions that compromise or even question church teachings, even outside of their official school functions, under threat of dismissal. I do not question his sincerity in trying to require this. I greatly fear for the church, however, because none of his colleagues will speak the truth to him about it.

Do his actions reflect the church's tradition of respect for the sanctity of a person's conscience, even a teacher in a Catholic school? Where are this fellow's fellow bishops in challenging him on such a divisive and intimidating dictum? Their silence is just as ugly as His Excellency's overbearing manipulations.

The Vatican recently permitted a bishop to remain in office after his conviction of criminal charges for shielding a priest who was a threat to children. I most certainly do question the sincerity of this unbelievable and unconscionable decision by the Vatican not to demand this bishop's removal. Does this reflect the church's pledge to strive for 100 percent protection of children? Where are the cardinals, archbishops, and bishops challenging the Vatican on such a "non-decision"? Why did Pope Francis let this happen? Their collective silence is shocking.

Indeed, with just these few examples (of course the list is much longer) any objective observer has to admit at least to a perception of disingenuousness on the part of the institutional church. But, even if it is just a perception, it is not acceptable for a church that is called to be a witness to Jesus' teachings and to be in loving service to the faith community.

• • • • • •

We begin to be truly Christian only when we embrace the Mystery of Jesus and his message with unconditional love in a personal relationship that begins and never ends with the Lord and Giver of Life.

• • • • • •

What I have realized is that we cannot wait for our church leaders to act. We must do so ourselves, and that is why I have written this book and why I have written others. I am old and getting older fast. I have less to lose. So it is easier for me to speak out. But you must do so as well.

Jesus gave us, his People of God, his church, one thing: hope. That hope is contained in the Holy Spirit he bestowed upon *all* his followers. The Holy Spirit, however, does not bring closure to disagreements, tensions, and challenges within the structures of our evolving church. For those of us with hope, closure is of no big consequence. For those with hope, we believe that the kingdom will come on earth, just as it has already come in heaven. That's Christian closure.

As paradoxical as it may seem, for us Catholic Christians closure is only possible when we embrace a new beginning. We begin to be truly Christian only when we embrace the Mystery of Jesus and his message with unconditional love in a personal relationship that begins and never ends with the Lord and Giver of Life. The rest, truly, is window dressing.

As I bring this book to an end, I am convinced that we the faithful must not walk away from Jesus' church, no matter what difficulties we may have with its practices, doctrines, and leaders. It is not yet known if the path Pope Francis is leading us on will effectively transform the institutional church in meaningful and long-lasting ways. Cardinal Walter Kasper realistically assesses this present time in the church's history in his book, *Pope Francis' Revolution of Tenderness and Love*. He asks if Pope Francis' pontificate will "…remain only a brief interlude in the church's history?" He further observes: "The challenge of this pontificate is far more radical than most suspect. It is a challenge for conservatives, who don't want to let themselves be surprised any more by God and who resist reforms, just as it is for progressives, who expect feasible, concrete solutions right here and now."

I believe that Jesus gifted the People of God with the Holy Spirit because he wanted all his faithful followers to take on the mission he began. The Spirit does not lead us to repeat the past. We are called to flourish and grow as we journey together with a faith that is always *becoming*, a faith that *will be* love for all those we encounter.

I dream of a church in which the Christian Tradition is not a repetition of a past but a creating of a future with Jesus' love that "was," "is now," and "will be" forever. I dream of a church in which the Christian Tradition means that Jesus is living in the hearts of the People of God right now, today. And I dream of a tomorrow in which the Holy Spirit enkindles in us the fire of God's love and we will be recreated. My final prayer is the daily prayer of my De LaSalle brothers: *Live, Jesus, in our hearts forever!*

A Creed to Live By...but Also Beyond

• • • • • •

A truly good book teaches me better than to read it.
I must soon lay it down, and commence living on its hint.
What I began by reading, I must finish by acting.

HENRY DAVID THOREAU

• • • • • •

The *Nicene Creed* is recited throughout the Catholic world as an expression of the professed faith of all its members. The time has come for me to act by renewing my statement of beliefs as a Catholic in light of the signs of the times. So, with true humility I offer the following:

I believe in one God, the Father almighty, maker of heaven and earth, of all things visible and invisible.

But I must go beyond this belief. The one, true, and invisible God is also our Mother, Brother, and Sister as we imagine our Maker's loving embrace of all. I, too, must embrace all people with love, especially the ones I least understand or agree with.

I believe in one Lord Jesus Christ, the Only Begotten Son of God, born of the Father before all ages. God from God, Light from Light, true God from true God, begotten not made, consubstantial with the Father; through him all things were made.

But I must go beyond this belief. Our God has not ended Creation. Our God continues to reveal the mystery of love in the hearts of the faithful and opens our minds to see truth through the light that shines from the world's multiplicity of cultures, ideas, and persons. I must encourage our church to be open and in dialogue with the kaleidoscopic array of diversity among all peoples of the world.

For us men and for our salvation, he came down from heaven, and by the Holy Spirit was incarnate of the Virgin Mary, and became man.

But I must go beyond this belief. I must stop referring to God as a male and to humanity as "mankind." Both are inaccurate and therefore misleading. Jesus became a human person, which makes all women and men equal in God's image and likeness. I must not tolerate within myself or my church gender prejudice of any kind, even in the name of improper translation!

For our sake he was crucified under Pontius Pilate, suffered death and was buried, and rose again on the third day in accordance with the Scriptures. He ascended into heaven and is seated at the right hand of the Father. He will come again in glory to judge the living and the dead, and his kingdom will have no end.

But I must go beyond this belief. It is we, the faithful women and men who are now the Mystical Body of the Risen Christ, who must bring his love to all. All women and men are totally equal as persons to serve the church, without any exceptions or exclusions. Jesus did not suffer the cross just for the many, and certainly not just for the already righteous. Jesus suffered, died, rose from the dead, and ascended into heaven for all us sinners. I must do whatever I can to support inclusion for all and at all times throughout our Catholic Church and in unity with all people of good will throughout the world, no matter what their religious beliefs or practices.

I believe in the Holy Spirit, the Lord, the giver of life, who proceeds from the Father and the Son, who with the Father and the Son is adored and glorified, who has spoken through the prophets. I believe in one, holy, catholic, and apostolic church. I confess one Baptism for the forgiveness of sins, and I look forward to the resurrection of the dead and the life of the world to come.

But I must go beyond this belief. I believe in Jesus' church as the People of God, not just as an institution with hierarchical positions. I must insist that all leaders in the church serve everyone in love, mercy, and compassion and never command with controls, exclusions, and harshness. I must always act with faith and zeal to make Jesus live in my heart forever by practicing his unconditional love for all. And I must look forward not only to heaven but also to the life of this world, which is the kingdom of God that is still to come "on earth, as it is in heaven."

Amen.

Amen.

RELATED TITLES

THE SILENT SCHISM
Listening to the Lived Experience of the Faithful
Brother Louis DeThomasis, FSC, and Sister Cynthia Nienhaus, CSA

Brother Louis De Thomasis and Sr. Cynthia Nienhaus use Pope Francis' "grammar of simplicity" to describe the current schism happening in the Catholic Church worldwide and to offer solutions for how to heal it. They call on both traditionalists and progressives in the church to recapture the mission of Jesus to bring about the reign of God "on earth, as it is in heaven." (128 pages, paperback)

FLYING IN THE FACE OF TRADITION
Listening to the Lived Experience of the Faithful
Brother Louis DeThomasis, FSC

Explores the Catholic notion of "tradition" as a source of revelation as a way out of the current quandary in the Catholic Church. (102 pages, paperback and hardcover)

DYNAMICS OF CATHOLIC EDUCATION
Letting the Catholic School Be School
Brother Louis DeThomasis, FSC

Addresses the important role of Catholic education in spreading the Christian message to new generations in new ways. (144 pages, paperback)

AN IRREPRESSIBLE HOPE
Notes from Chicago Catholics
Edited by Claire Bushey, Artwork by Franklin McMahon

Stories, essays, poems, and passionate personal pleas by more than thirty Chicago Catholics on their hopes for the church. (84 pages, paperback)

Available from booksellers or call 800-397-2282
www.actapublications.com